DANCING WITH THE *Divine*

Six Dance Lessons to Free Your Inner Spirit and Live an Extraordinary Life

JULIE A. VANCE

Copyright ©2022 by Julie A. Vance

New Cumberland, Pennsylvania

All rights reserved. No part of this book may be reproduced, distributed, or transmitted in any form or by any means, including photocopying, recording, or other electronic or mechanical methods, without the prior written permission of the publisher, except in the case of brief quotations embodied in critical articles, reviews, and certain other noncommercial uses permitted by copyright law. This book is not intended to serve as a replacement for therapy or medical advice.

Cover design by BrandKore™

Printed in the United States of America
ISBN: 978-1-7378408-0-0
Library of Congress Control Number: 2022904744

*To the divine presence that is always
leading me in the dance of life*

Contents

Introduction: The Incredible Power Within 1

Part One: A Vision of Dancing with the Divine 11
   1. Ordination Day.. 15

Part Two: Preparation for the Dance 25
   2. Following the Rules.. 29
   3. Going Within.. 49
   4. Moving Through Transition 69

Part Three: Dance Lessons 89
   5. Leading and Following... 93
   6. Releasing the Imprisoned Splendor.......................... 115
   7. Flowing with Divine Timing...................................... 137
   8. It's All About Trust 157
   9. One Step at a Time—Moving from Fear to Faith.... 179
   10. Keep On Keeping On 201

Part Four: Living the Dance.................................... 223
   11. The Dance Continues 227

About the Author 249

Gratitude and Appreciation 251

Introduction

The Incredible Power Within

What if you knew you had an incredible power—a power that is with you twenty-four hours a day, seven days a week, 365 days a year—encouraging you, inspiring you, guiding you? What if you could learn to access, trust, and follow that power in every choice you make? What if you could transform the self-doubt and fear you experience—more often than you like to admit—into clarity, confidence, and courage?

I believe that each one of us does have that power within us. It is the voice of Spirit, God, the Universe—whatever you choose to call it—individualized as your own inner spirit. And I *know* it is possible to learn to recognize, trust, and follow our inner spirit in every choice we make. How do I know this? I know through my own personal journey from being an outer-directed, follow-the-rules person, to being an inner-directed, trust-my-innate-wisdom person. I know through helping thousands of individuals in my career as a minister, teacher, workshop facilitator, and spiritual counselor for more than thirty years. I know that trusting our inner spirit has brought greater peace, freedom, clarity, confidence, and courage to me and to those who have learned to free their inner spirit. In the words of students in my Trusting Your Inner Spirit classes:

> Since learning to trust my inner spirit, I feel a slowing down inside myself. I am calmer in situations of heightened anxiety or tension.
> When I follow my inner spirit, I feel at peace.
> When I follow my inner spirit, I feel free. I am reminded that I have limitless access to the power of the Universe.
> When I follow my inner spirit, I feel and express the love, peace, wisdom, and joy that I am. I don't have to worry about what to say or do. I feel more confident and creative, and I have less need to be "right."

Discovering My Inner Spirit

I discovered my inner spirit in the early 1980s when I began attending a Unity church, "a positive path for spiritual living." I was awed by the fact that the co-founders of Unity, Charles and Myrtle Fillmore, relied on their inner spirit to direct them in all choices they made. They were not deterred by a seeming lack of money, resources, or energy. They simply trusted that if they listened to this inner wisdom and followed it without question, everything they needed would be provided. And so it was!

Somewhere in my rational, practical mind, this idea resonated with me, and I began to apply it in my life. I discovered how to access my inner spirit and began to follow its promptings, first in little things, like "read this book" or "call this person," and ultimately in the big decisions of my life, such as leaving my eighteen-year teaching position without knowing what I was going to do next or applying to be a Unity minister after resisting the idea for over twenty years.

Eventually, I realized that listening to and following my inner spirit had become the guiding principle in my life, and I was embarking on a journey that I had never imagined when I began the process. I was making choices, taking steps, stepping out in faith, and learning that everything I need to know is inside me—that I have an inner voice providing guidance that is perfect for me, at the right time, in the right way. I was becoming less dependent on rules and shoulds and more confident in the choices I was making, more at peace with myself, and more in the flow of life. This journey of discovering and following my inner spirit has been the most exciting adventure I have ever undertaken.

In the 1990s, I began ballroom dancing and discovered that many of the lessons I was learning in ballroom dancing mirrored those I was learning on my spiritual journey. Since I loved dancing, I began to use the phrase "dancing with the Divine" to signify the process of listening to and following guidance. To me, dancing with the Divine means knowing that there's a divine presence, a divine partner—our inner spirit—ever moving us in the direction of our highest good.

As I look back at my life, I see that although I wasn't consciously aware of it for many years, I was always dancing with the Divine. But it wasn't until the day I was ordained as a Unity minister in 2005 that I experienced the coming together of these two great passions in my life: my spiritual journey and ballroom dancing.

WRITING THIS BOOK

Have you ever noticed that sometimes seeds are planted in you—seeds that take months or even years to bear fruit in your life?

On my ordination day, the seed for this book was planted in my heart and soul. Even so, thirteen years later, when I finally began to write this book, I doubted myself. Did my inner spirit really want me to write this book? Why me? Why now? And if the book truly was divinely guided, why wasn't the writing flowing?

I turned to my inner spirit for answers to these questions and for guidance on how to proceed, using the process of dialoguing with my inner spirit, a technique I often use when I encounter doubt or fear. I'm sharing this dialogue, "A Conversation with My Inner Spirit," for several reasons:

- As an example of a process I find helpful in connecting with my inner spirit.
- To let you know that no matter how committed you are to following your inner spirit, sometimes—especially when you're stepping out of your comfort zone—you may have doubts and fears, and that's okay.
- Because I felt my inner spirit guiding me to share the conversation. (And after all, this is a book about trusting our inner spirit.)

In the dialogue, even though my inner spirit is a part of me, I differentiate between my human self (Julie) and my divine self (inner spirit).

A Conversation with My Inner Spirit

JULIE: I thought writing a book about dancing with the Divine would be easy, that it would flow from you, through me—after all, isn't that what's supposed to happen when one dances with the Divine? It's supposed to be smooth and flowing like that beautiful waltz I danced at my ordination. Why then am I struggling to write—to find the words to express what's in my heart? I know that you have something to say through me. You've been guiding me to write a book for years. You've given me the title and told me it's to be about dancing with you in my spiritual life and dancing with a human partner in ballroom dancing. So what is it that I'm not hearing? Am I trying too hard to make it happen? What do I need to do to allow the words to flow through me?

INNER SPIRIT: *I want you to be still and listen. I want you to hear what I am saying. I long to speak through you. You must get out of the way and let me lead. Remember, the most beautiful waltz is danced when one person leads and one person follows.*

JULIE: Can you tell me this in practical, everyday language? How do I let you lead me in writing this book?

INNER SPIRIT: *First you set your intention: "Let me write from the heart the words you want me to share." Then you choose the topic for the day as guided or as the energy of the moment is leading you. It may be one of the topics you have already listed or one that occurs to you in the moment. Then you listen and, just as you write in your journal, write or type whatever comes to you to say.*

JULIE: What about all the notes I have on the topics?

INNER SPIRIT: *In a dance, you learn the steps, then you put them together into patterns, and then you listen to the music. There is, at some point, a coming together of the steps, the patterns, the feeling, and the music, and you are doing a dance. The dance is dancing you. You become one with the dance. When you dance with the Divine, you set your intention, you listen, you follow, and you no longer know which is Spirit and which is you. They're not separate. They are one. You and Spirit are one just as you and your human partner are one in the dance.*

The feeling of oneness doesn't always happen at first. It takes practice and commitment to staying with the process, but if you persist, it happens. Writing a book can be like that. Sometimes you're caught up in the steps and aren't seeing the bigger picture.

Spirit sees the bigger picture, and as you persist, you will see the bigger picture too. It's a process, and the process is important. What you'll learn in writing this book is what's important. If you persist and stay with the process, you will benefit greatly. No doubt others will benefit as well. We will learn this dance together, and we will master it.

After this dialogue, I felt a sense of peace, of confidence, and of trust. I knew that I was the right person to write this book and that I would be guided each step of the way.

Day by day, as I continued to write, I was led to dig deeper and uncover the self-limiting ideas and beliefs that kept me from fully trusting my inner spirit. (Yes, I am still in the process of learning to trust my inner spirit completely.) As I journaled, dialogued, and practiced the "dance steps" you'll find in this book, I was able to free my inner spirit from many of these self-limiting beliefs and ideas: *Who am I to write a book? How will I know what to include in my book? Isn't my life too ordinary to share in a book?* In reviewing my life and the lessons I'd learned, I was reminded of how extraordinary an ordinary life can be when we trust our inner spirit to guide us.

READING THIS BOOK

Are you ready to free your inner spirit and live an extraordinary life? In this book, I am inviting you to discover how to recognize, trust, and follow the incredible power within you—the power of your inner spirit—so that you can dance with the Divine with clarity, confidence, courage, and joy.

During my twenty-five years of ministry—which has included delivering thousands of Sunday messages—I've been told over and over again by congregants and friends that they enjoy hearing stories and examples from my life and the lives of others to illustrate the ideas I present, as well as practical steps to integrate the lessons into their lives. I've taken the same approach with this book. As you read it, you'll learn about my journey in recognizing, trusting, and following my inner spirit's guidance. In the pages ahead, I share the insights I've gained about how this process works and the tools that have been helpful to me and to those I've taught and worked with over the years. You'll also find the lessons I've learned in ballroom dancing, an integral part of my journey, interspersed throughout this book. Whether or not you've ever set foot on a dance floor or had any desire to learn ballroom dancing, the dance lessons are universal and can be applied to any area of your life.

The book is divided into four parts:

- *A Vision of Dancing with the Divine:* As you read about a special day in my life when two great passions—my spiritual journey and ballroom dancing—came together in a beautiful dance with the Divine, you'll discover what life can look and feel like when you trust and follow your inner spirit and everything comes together in perfect harmony.

- *Preparation for the Dance:* As I relate ballroom dancing to periods of spiritual growth, you'll learn tools to recognize, listen to, and follow your own inner spirit.
- *Dance Lessons:* As I share six lessons I've learned in ballroom dancing, you'll learn to apply each lesson to your journey of learning to recognize, trust, and follow your inner spirit.
- *Living the Dance:* This part of the book summarizes the steps in learning to trust and follow your inner spirit, invites you to reflect on what you've learned on your journey, and offers an opportunity, through meditation, to experience the feeling of dancing with the Divine.

An Invitation

Although I may not personally know you or your unique dance with the Divine, I do know this: you have all the answers you need inside yourself. You have an incredible power within you—the power of your inner spirit—willing to encourage you, guide you, inspire you. You can learn to recognize, trust, and follow your inner spirit in every choice you make.

I invite you to join me in this journey, and I truly believe that as you read this book and practice the "dance steps" to assist you in getting more in touch with your inner spirit, your dance with the Divine will bring you greater clarity, confidence, courage, and peace of mind and heart as well as a deeper sense of connection with your inner spirit.

Are you willing to free your inner spirit and live an extraordinary life?

If you are ready and willing, turn the page and begin the dance!

Part One

A Vision of Dancing with the Divine

To watch us dance is to hear our hearts speak.

– Hopi Indian saying

    When you follow your inner spirit, there is a flow to your life—a feeling of harmony and balance. My ordination day and the events leading up to it are examples of this flow. On the special day when I was ordained as a Unity minister, I experienced the coming together, in perfect harmony, of two great passions in my life—ballroom dancing and my spiritual journey of learning to follow my inner spirit—in a beautiful dance with the Divine.

    The vision of this day—a seed planted in my consciousness by my inner spirit—blossomed into one of the most memorable days of my life. I wonder what vision your inner spirit wants to plant in your mind and heart. As you read the story of my ordination day, may it inspire you to listen to the voice of your own inner spirit.

Chapter 1

Ordination Day

April 10, 2005

Arm in arm, my partner and I enter the ballroom—Gary in a black silk button-down vest and me in a flowing black-and-white feathered low-back ball gown. Our DJ for the evening, Tom Albert, announces to my congregation, family, and friends, "It's Gary Edwards and the other one! It's her! It's Reverend Julie!"

I can feel the excitement in the air and see the faces gazing wide-eyed at me as, for the first time, they see their newly ordained minister transformed from the spiritual leader who, just two hours earlier, solemnly spoke her ordination vows—dressed in a conservative, pale pink high-necked, button-down suit—to a woman they barely recognize.

As Gary and I take our places on the dance floor, the hauntingly beautiful music begins—the theme from *The Thorn Birds,* one of my favorite movies. With 125 pairs of eyes focused on us, we begin the waltz routine we've practiced hundreds of times, so often that we could probably dance it in our dreams. But today something is different, almost magical. We glide across the room, my gown swirling around me as Gary leads me in the underarm turns. I feel as if I'm dancing on air—in harmony with myself, my partner, and everyone in the room. Gone are the self-doubt and fear I often feel when performing a dance routine. The dance feels graceful and effortless. I feel free, confident, and at ease. Today I am dancing with Gary, my human partner, but I feel as though I am also dancing with the Divine. We are both dancing with the Divine!

A Seed Is Planted

Months earlier, the idea of dancing on my ordination day began as a tiny seed planted in my consciousness by my inner spirit. (I believe that our inner spirit often whispers ideas into our ears when we least expect them.) At first, when members of my congregation asked me how I wanted to celebrate my ordination day, I'd thought of a simple reception in the church's social room following the ordination ceremony upstairs in the sanctuary. (Somewhat boring, but practical.)

However, as I was driving to church one day (lots of divine ideas seem to come to me on my thirty-minute drives to church), I heard my inner spirit say, *"Your congregation would love to see you dance! Why not have a dinner reception and perform a ballroom dance following the dinner?"*

What a creative idea—to be able to share my love of ballroom dancing with my congregation on one of the most important days of my life! Definitely something to think about.

A few days later, I read this affirmation in *Science of Mind* magazine: "I dance with the Divine in me, and it is beautiful!" This seemed too coincidental not to be a sign from my inner spirit. In that moment, the theme for my ordination day was born: "Dancing with the Divine."

This was the first time I used this phrase, which to me has become synonymous with trusting and following my inner spirit. I could imagine myself expressing this theme in two ways on my ordination day: first, at my ordination ceremony, sharing in words the story of how my dance with the Divine had led me to become a Unity minister. Then, at my reception, sharing in dance—with my dance partner—the physical representation of dancing with the Divine.

THE SEED BLOSSOMS

When I shared my vision with my council and members of my congregation, they loved the idea of a ceremony at our church followed by a dinner reception and ballroom dance presentation.

The question was: Where in the small town of Palmyra, Pennsylvania—where the church was located—could we find a venue close to the church where we could not only have a catered dinner but a space large enough to perform a ballroom dance?

And with all my responsibilities in the church, as well as preparing for the ordination service, who would organize the reception?

Because this idea had been inspired by my inner spirit, I knew that if I trusted it to guide me and followed that guidance one step at a time, everything I needed would be provided: the ideas, the resources, the time, the money…all of it. And it was!

The next week, my friend Sharon, a skilled event organizer, offered me a wonderful ordination gift: to organize my reception. She would find the venue, create the invitations and decorations, and organize a team of church members to assist in the planning. And she told me, "You can be as involved as you want to be. Let me know what you want, and I'll take care of it." This was exactly what I wanted to hear and a demonstration of my inner spirit providing exactly what I needed.

The first step was to find the venue. Despite making many phone calls, Sharon found no viable possibilities; however, I suddenly remembered a high school dance I had attended at the Treadway Inn in Lebanon, about twenty minutes from the church. I hadn't thought about this in years. Was the hotel still there? It was—now the Lebanon Best Western Inn. When Sharon called the venue, she confirmed that we could have a catered dinner there, the date was available, and there was a real ballroom dance floor. Although I'd been skeptical at first (sometimes I second-guess the wisdom of my inner spirt), I was now very excited about performing a dance routine. I was sure this was a sign that we were being divinely guided in planning this event.

Three-Step Process

Dancing with the Divine is a three-step process of co-creating: We ask, listen, and then follow the guidance we receive. So, in planning for my ordination service, I asked how I could create an experience for myself, my congregation, and all who would attend that would allow us all to feel as though we were part of the dance of the Divine bringing us to that moment. As I listened to my inner spirit, I heard that the day was to include three elements:

- My dance with the Divine that had brought me to this day of commitment through ordination
- The dance of my congregation, family, and friends that had brought them to this day of sharing in my commitment through ordination
- The physical representation of dancing with the Divine through the medium of ballroom dance

How would these three elements all come together in a day that flowed like a dance? It was now my task to continue listening to the guidance I received and to follow it one step at a time.

Fulfillment of the Vision

After much planning, preparation, and listening, the day finally arrived. Sunday, April 10 at 2:00 p.m., I entered my church's sanctuary to the sounds of Bach's "Prelude in E Major." What a thrill it was to see the church filled with friends, family, and members of my congregation who had supported me for the last four years as I completed the requirements to become an ordained Unity minister! As I took my seat in the front row beside my sponsoring minister, I whispered in her ear, "I can't believe that this day is finally here! Sixty minutes from now, I'm really going to be an ordained minister at last!" I closed my eyes and said a quick prayer that this day truly would feel like a dance with the Divine, not only for me but for those who had come to share this time with me.

Everything seemed to unfold perfectly that day, or as we say in Unity, "in perfect divine order." The service began with the congregation reading the opening statement, which set the theme for the day's events: "I dance with the Divine in me, and it is beautiful!" How powerful those words felt to me as I heard them affirmed for me by over a hundred very special people in my life! Throughout the ceremony, colleagues and friends shared memories of our work together in the Palmyra community and our growth as a congregation. Even the music reflected significant moments in the life of our church and in our dance as a congregation: from "On Holy Ground" (reminiscent of the first Sunday in our new church in 2001) to the earth-shattering notes of "Upon This Rock" (first sung at our church building's 100th anniversary celebration in 2002.)

I was delighted to receive a stole (a narrow band sometimes worn around the neck by clergy) created by the children of Unity of Palmyra with symbols and pictures representing our church. Not only was it special to me because the children had created it for me but also because I'd forgotten to bring the stole I'd planned to wear. As I slipped on the beautiful stole that had been so lovingly created for me, my first words were, "So, that's why I forgot to wear my stole today!" (Sometimes even in forgetting, our inner spirit is guiding us.)

Usually, a minister chooses not to share the message at their own ordination, but I was determined to let go of any rules or shoulds and focus on what felt right for me. I'd always shared parts of my journey with my congregation in my Sunday messages, and I felt confident that on this day my inner spirit was leading me to share my journey in dancing with the Divine that had led me to this moment.

I began with these words:

> One morning this week, I asked for divine inspiration on the thoughts to share with you today. I went downstairs and had my morning cup of tea, and there on the teabag was a message that said, "The whole universe is a stage on which your mind dances with your body, guided by your heart." (Imagine—instantaneous inspiration on a teabag!) That quote expresses to me the sense of harmony—of oneness—of being in the flow of life that we experience when we dance with the Divine.

I continued to share my dance with the Divine in words, likening it to dancing with a human partner when one person leads and the other follows, where the dance unfolds one step at a time until the desired result is obtained or the dance is complete.

The service was concluded with the rite of ordination. Before my congregation, family, and friends, I affirmed my commitment to my calling to ministry. Tears filled my eyes as I received a standing ovation and could see and feel the love expressed by my congregation, family, and friends.

As we all stood, joined hands, and sang "Let There Be Peace on Earth," the traditional ending for a Unity service, I watched everyone swaying from side to side in time with the music in what I can only describe as a joyful dance of oneness.

I had completed sharing, in words, my journey of dancing with the Divine that led to my ordination day. Now it was time to head to the reception to share my journey through dance.

When I entered the reception ballroom, I immediately noticed the tables decorated in ribbons of blue, turquoise, and aqua as well as the white candles in glass holders with glittery stones of blue, silver, and green—my favorite colors. DJ Tom was even wearing a sparkly silver jacket! My friends, family, and congregation were seated and looking up at me with smiles and questions in their eyes: On this day of dancing with the Divine, what's going to happen next?

After a few minutes of greeting the guests, it was time to begin our meal. DJ Tom—in his usual fun-loving, offbeat style—introduced me with a drum roll and the words, "Here's Julie!" to which I responded, "That's some introduction for a prayer!"

After the meal, the guests were invited to participate in the dance. In addition to ballroom-dance music, there was also freestyle, the electric slide (for those who liked line dances), and even the chicken dance. The guests were encouraged to "get up and dance; and if you don't think you can dance, do it anyway!" After all, this was a day of dancing! I loved seeing so many people relaxing and having a good time on the dance floor.

Finally, it was time for the long-awaited moment when the guests would see me and my partner dance for the first time. As the guests returned to their seats, their attention was focused on me and Gary as we stood at the entrance to the ballroom. The music played, and we began to dance. Through the spin turns and twinkles and the elegant rise and fall of the waltz, we glided across the floor. The three-minute routine seemed much too short for me. I felt I could have danced all night.

As the last notes of the theme from *The Thorn Birds* sounded and we took our bows, for a moment there was silence in the ballroom. Then everyone in the room began to shout and cheer, encouraged by DJ Tom, who called out, "That was the applause for the outfit. Now let's hear it for Reverend Julie!" I could feel the love and support for me, just as I had when I took my ordination vows.

There was still more to come. Gary and I danced a second dance. To balance the elegance and grace of the waltz—and because dancing with the Divine has many facets—we chose a hustle: a dynamic, flashy, and powerful disco dance. As if seeing their minister in a ballgown wasn't shocking enough for my congregation, for this dance, I wore a hot pink, cross-bodice, low-back, pleated-skirt costume—definitely not the attire they usually saw me wear. The routine was fun, fast, and full of energy. After this dance, my audience looked even more amazed than during the waltz routine.

The reception ended with more dancing for everyone and best wishes for me as the guests began to leave. Any question I may have had about my congregation feeling part of the dance that day was answered with a comment by one of the guests: "Today my heart danced with you!"

Now, years later, when I question the wisdom of my inner spirit or hesitate to trust its guidance—which I sometimes still do—I remember my ordination day and how it felt to dance with the Divine. I know that I want to experience that feeling of joy, ease, and confidence more and more in my life.

Fortunately, my entire ordination day went as smoothly as I'd hoped it would; however, the path leading to this day—my life journey—definitely did not always flow like a beautiful waltz. Like any life journey, it had its ups and downs, twists and turns. But step by step, I found my way from self-doubt and fear to recognizing and trusting my inner spirit and learning to dance with the Divine. I began to see that every part of my life contained lessons that contributed to my growth and unfoldment.

As you follow my journey, I invite you to reflect on your own pathway through life and to discover the lessons that have helped you experience greater clarity, confidence, and courage.

Part Two

Preparation for the Dance

We learn by practice. Whether it means to learn to dance by practicing dancing or to learn to live by practicing living, the principles are the same. One becomes in some area an athlete of God.

– Martha Graham

Just as in dancing there are rules to learn before the actual dancing begins, so there are rules we learn when we begin our lives on this earth—rules we learn from our parents, from our teachers, from our peers, and from life itself—before we can fully participate in our dance with the Divine. Some of these rules may need to be modified or forgotten as we begin to make choices that honor who we are. Others may serve us well throughout our lives.

As I continued on my life journey, I learned that there was something more than rules and outer direction to guide me. I discovered within myself an internal guidance system—my connection with the divine presence—my inner spirit. I began to learn how to access, recognize, and trust this inner spirit to guide me in the experiences of my life. When I was able to do this, I felt greater clarity, confidence, and courage in making choices that felt right to me.

Although I believe that my dance with the Divine began with my birth—or maybe even before that—it wasn't until I consciously chose to trust and follow my inner spirit that I began to understand what it meant to dance with the Divine in my life.

How do we move from being an outer-directed person dependent on following the rules and shoulds of life to being an inner-directed person who trusts and follows our inner spirit? We do it one step at a time.

Your path will be different from mine, but as you read about the steps I took in learning to trust my inner spirit, you may glean insights that will guide you in dancing with the Divine in your life.

Chapter 2

Following the Rules

As a child, I loved to dance. I have a picture of myself at about five years old wearing a green plaid dress and black patent leather Mary Jane shoes, whirling around the living room with an expression of pure joy on my face. Although it has been many years since that picture was taken, I remember the feeling of freedom I felt when I danced like that—uninhibited, joyful, spontaneous, free. No rules, no expectations, just moving to the music inside me. Although I didn't know it at the time, I think it may have been one of my first experiences of dancing with the Divine.

Are we born knowing how to dance with the Divine, to trust our inner spirit? Maybe so. If all the answers we need are inside us—and I believe they are—then somewhere deep inside ourselves, we know how to create the feeling of freedom, joy, and confidence we long for. For me, dancing has been a way of connecting with the Divine spirit within me, and it has been a constant, in one form or another, throughout my life.

LEARNING THE RULES

But…do we learn to trust our inner spirit as part of our education at home, at school, in our daily activities? Do our early life experiences create that sense of freedom I felt through dancing? Unless your childhood and early adulthood were very different from mine, I don't think so. Most of us learn to follow rules and adapt to outer structures that are designed to establish order in our lives but which often deprive us of creativity and a sense of freedom.

In my early years—and for most of my life—I rarely felt the sense of freedom I experienced when dancing. I was a serious, sensitive child who was very good at learning and following rules and expectations of others, and it seemed as though there were lots of them—from parents, teachers, neighbors, peers, life itself.

I wanted to be a perfect little girl. I wasn't sure what perfect was, but I believed that if I just followed the rules, I could be good enough, smart enough, and popular enough to be accepted and loved.

The trouble was that sometimes the rules weren't consistent and I didn't know which ones to follow. From my mother, I learned many shoulds and shouldn'ts—you should pretend you like someone, even if you don't; you shouldn't say how you feel if it would offend someone; you should always be pleasant and smile, even if you're annoyed or angry.

Much to my mother's chagrin, my dad did not always follow these shoulds. At our family picnics, instead of engaging in endless small talk with the guests after he completed barbecuing the chicken or grilling the hamburgers, he'd find a chair apart from the crowd and sit quietly or even read the Sunday newspaper. Instead of politely agreeing with what was said, he would often—in his gruff but tender manner—state exactly the opposite opinion. Because I observed that these "socially unacceptable" behaviors embarrassed my mother, I learned to become embarrassed by them as well. When I think about my dad's propensity to be true to himself, I realize our guests were not offended but concluded it was "just Ammon being himself." Maybe it gave them the freedom to be themselves. And maybe it was a catalyst for me when I began to question the shoulds that would sometimes seem to control my life. In the early years of my life, however, I tried to follow the shoulds my mother taught me, and I became very skillful at hiding my feelings from others.

Have you every noticed that sometimes, years later, these early learnings come back to haunt you?

Masked Emotions

In the 1990s, when I was leading a self-esteem retreat at Warm Springs Lodge in Pennsylvania, one of the participants noticed that I was practicing the ability to hide my feelings. We'd been discussing the masks we wear—the ways we hide our feelings and our vulnerability from others. For instance, we might choose the mask of the clown, covering up our feelings of sadness with laughter or jokes, or we might portray Mr. Nice Guy or Ms. Nice Gal, agreeing with others when we really feel just the opposite.

We'd been in session for several hours, and it was time for a break. It was a beautiful day, and some of the participants chose to go outside on the deck. At the end of the fifteen-minute break, about eight people were chatting and enjoying the warm sunshine outdoors and didn't hear me when I called for them to come back inside.

I stepped outside and called to them, "It's time to come inside and resume our session."

No response.

"The break is over. Let's come inside and get started."

No response.

After several attempts to capture their attention, I felt my smile faltering and my shoulders tightening.

When we finally returned to our circle of sharing, one young woman, recalling our conversation on masks, asked me, "Did you realize you were smiling even though you were angry?"

I hadn't realized I was doing this, but I had unwittingly unveiled one of my masks. After that experience, I began to pay attention to times when I was hiding my anger or fear under a confident, self-assured mask. It became a clear sign to me that I was following a should instead of being true to myself.

As I learned to follow my inner spirit, I realized that shoulds weren't the language of my inner spirit and were an invitation to ask myself, "Who said so? What do I believe? What feels right for me in this situation?"

Unspoken Rules

Not all rules or expectations are stated out loud. Maybe because I was an only child or because I was shy and sensitive, my parents—especially my mother—were overly protective of me. One of the unspoken rules I learned was, "If you want to be safe, stay close to your mother; don't venture too far out of your comfort zone" (or, more appropriately, the comfort zone of your mother).

Staying close to my mother became a problem when it was time for me to go to school. On my first day at Henry Houck Elementary School, leaving my mother to enter a classroom filled with a teacher and thirty children I didn't know felt overwhelming to me. I cried, held firmly to my mother's hand, and refused to enter the classroom. Fortunately, my teacher was able to persuade my mother to leave and me to enter the classroom, albeit with some trepidation on my part. Somehow, I made it through the first weeks of school and actually began to enjoy the learning process. I also learned that I could be safe without staying close to my mother every minute of the day.

Most of the rules I learned in school—be quiet, sit still, listen to the teacher, do your homework—were easy for me to follow. But in first grade, I learned what happens when you don't follow the rules.

Broken Rules

I am sitting at my '50s-style wooden desk, carefully writing numbers from one to 100 on a paper with exactly 100 squares on it—one number in each square. I finish with ninety-nine numbers when I hear the bell clanging for recess time. Eager for a break from this tedious task, I rush out to the playground, leaving one number to be completed when I come back inside.

After recess, I return to my desk to complete my assignment when I see Miss Nichols, standing by my desk, pointing to my unfinished work, and saying, "Julie, I said you were to finish your work before going out to recess." I see the other children staring at me in surprise. (I am known to be a child who always follows directions.)

I feel my cheeks turning red, tears welling up in my eyes. I ask myself: Didn't I hear Miss Nichols' direction to finish my work before I went out to recess? Was I in a hurry to get outside to play, or did I think that because I only had one more number to write, I could easily finish when I came in from recess?

Whatever the reason, I'm so embarrassed and ashamed that I want to put my head down on my desk and cry. But even at six years old, I have learned to hide my feelings, so I swallow my tears and pretend that the admonition didn't hurt my feelings.

Very quickly, I learned a new rule: "Finish your work before you go out to play."

I learned my lesson so well that throughout my school years, I always completed my homework as soon as I got home from school and before I went out to play. I wanted to be the perfect student. Looking back today, I wonder if the seed of learning that I couldn't trust myself to make the right choices was born that day.

Developing Our Inner Self

Although on my outer journey I was very good at following rules and expectations of others, from a very early age I was drawn within—thinking about the world, asking questions, dreaming.

Looking at a picture of me at six months old, my mother told me, "Even at a young age, you were a serious young lady." Looking at that picture today, I imagine myself thinking, "Hmm…I wonder: What is the meaning of this life journey I am embarking upon?"

In the early years, while we're developing our outer self—the self we show the world—we're also developing our inner self—the self that questions, dreams, and imagines all that we can do and be. For me, as an only child and one who was shy and introverted, I had lots of time and opportunity to develop my inner self.

At a very young age, I seemed to have a way of looking deeper within, of seeing beyond the surface of things, a skill that would later prove valuable on my inner journey. I learned to appreciate and enjoy times of quiet and solitude. For me, solitude was a quiet place within myself where I could think my own thoughts and be whoever I wanted to be in the moment—a place without rules or expectations where I was free to be myself.

I was often perfectly content to read a book, sit on a blanket outside, or swing on my swing set, singing songs I'd learned in Sunday school. I also started keeping a journal. This began as an account of my daily activities in my elementary school years but later became more focused on my feelings and thoughts. Eventually, through the years, journaling led me to insights and understandings about my purpose in life and a means of hearing the voice of my inner spirit.

I've come to believe that our inner spirit is always with us, patiently awaiting our recognition of it. Developing our inner self is the first step in coming to know that inner spirit.

Roots and Wings

As I reflect on my early years, I think about a quote often attributed to Dr. Jonas Salk (creator of the polio vaccine): "Good parents give their children roots and wings. Roots to know where home is and wings to fly away."

There is no doubt in my mind that my parents gave me strong roots. I felt cherished and loved by both of my parents, safe (even though sometimes overly protected), and instilled with solid values to live by and a sense of responsibility for myself and my life. My wings, though, seemed to come from within, from a connection with the inner spirit that I didn't yet recognize but with which I'd begun to connect in my times of solitude and silence.

As my spiritual awareness has grown, I've wondered if I've been motivated to spread my wings and follow my dreams through observing my parents' experience of having their wings clipped. My mother's parents told her that her dream of becoming an actress was no path for a respectable young woman. And my father's parents cited seven children and a lack of money as barriers to his dream of becoming a veterinarian.

Do you remember any of your childhood dreams? Maybe, like me, you had dreams for your life that felt natural to you, and you never doubted that you would achieve them. One of my dreams was to become a teacher. From the time I was in second grade, one of my favorite activities was playing school with my dolls or my neighborhood friends. I was always the teacher, and there was never any doubt in my mind that teaching was my destiny. I assisted in teaching Bible School and Sunday School in my junior high and high school years and organized games and parties for the younger children in my neighborhood. I liked to be in charge and to be the one to make the rules, but I soon learned that my playmates didn't always want to follow the rules that I set for them. Being in charge—or in control, as I think of it now—served me well in positions of leadership but not so well when learning to let go and follow my inner spirit.

During my school years, I was a conscientious student and found that doing well academically gave me a sense of confidence and greater ease in interacting with others. I had many friends and was involved in extracurricular activities, mostly relating to service, such as Tri-Hi-Y (a service organization) and FTA (Future Teachers of America). In my senior year, I participated in an oratorical contest along with six other contestants. I spoke about "The Will to Win," focused on the idea that with enough determination and persistence, we can achieve whatever we make up our minds to do.

Although I didn't win the contest, my determination and persistence in being on the stage in front of 300 fellow students and teachers was a huge accomplishment for the girl who had been afraid to leave her mother to go to school twelve years earlier. I was beginning to spread my wings and step out of my comfort zone.

QUESTIONING THE RULES

As we grow from childhood into adolescence and young adulthood, it's natural to begin to question some of the rules and expectations that are placed on us.

Although I excelled academically in high school, I was beginning to question some of the expectations placed on me. Early on, I was told I wasn't good at sports. Was this because in physical education class I failed to serve a volleyball into the opposing court five times in a row as required? Or to perform a ten-minute routine with Indian clubs (my hands and arms just couldn't seem to get into the proper positions)? Was I not considered creative because my artistic creations didn't look like the teacher's examples? I do know that these rigid and unrealistic expectations caused me to avoid sports for years because I felt I wasn't good enough to participate and to avoid any type of artistic endeavor because I thought I'd probably do it wrong. It took me years to understand that I was creative in many ways—writing, speaking, preparing a meal, simply being myself—and that I could enjoy a sport or physical activity without having to be the best or to meet someone else's expectations for me.

When I entered Millersville State College in the late 1960s, I discovered that living on campus provided its own set of rules to follow: having to be in my dormitory by 8:30 p.m. on weekdays (which, in light of the freedom that college students experience now, probably sounds like the Dark Ages), signing in and out whenever leaving campus, no boys allowed in the dormitory rooms. By this time, I had internalized many of the rules and shoulds from my early years, but I also became aware of expectations and rules others tried to impose on me. On my own for the first time, I think my college years were the beginning of my questioning what was right and wrong for me and developing an inner guidance system.

One evening in my freshman year, I'm invited to go with a group of girls to a fraternity party at Franklin and Marshall, a nearby liberal arts college. After a thirty-minute ride jammed into a car with six or seven other girls, we arrive at the fraternity house. When we enter the house, I see guys and girls sprawled on the couches, lounge chairs, or pillows on the floor. I see bottles of beer, tumblers filled with wine, and assorted bottles of whiskey, rum, and coke. I suspect that the brownies I see on a plate on the coffee table are laced with marijuana. Already feeling uncomfortable, wondering why in the world I let my friends talk me into coming to this party, and realizing I have no way of getting back to

Millersville until our driver is ready to leave, I look around for an uncluttered place to sit. One of the fraternity brothers motions for me to take a seat beside him on a tattered couch on the other side of the room. His speech is slurred when he asks me what I'd like to drink. When I hesitate, thinking I want to have my wits about me in this situation, he warns me, "If you want to be invited back, you have to drink."

I want to be cool, I want to be accepted, but as I look around the room, I think, "Who wants to come back here?" and I refuse the drink, opting for a bottle of Coca-Cola instead.

I discovered something very important about myself that night. Someone telling me what rules I had to follow to be popular made me feel the anger I often kept hidden, and awakened a rebellious aspect of myself, an aspect that, as time went by, I came to respect and admire.

Though I didn't always resist peer pressure in my college years, I did begin to say no to what didn't feel right to me and yes to what did.

BENEFITS OF FOLLOWING THE RULES

Are there benefits to following the rules? Of course there are. Many rules keep us safe and healthy. Although I didn't understand it at the time, I've come to believe that the rules and expectations I learned from parents, teachers, and peers are like training wheels on a bicycle. They give us structure and balance until we're ready and able to develop our own internal guidance system, to discern what works and what doesn't work in our lives. They're preparation for trusting our own inner spirit—for dancing with the Divine in our lives.

I would clearly see this analogy when I began taking ballroom dance lessons in the early 1990s. Eager to emulate the seasoned couples in their dazzling ball gowns and elegant tuxedos gliding across the floor, I was disheartened to find that before I could even hope to look like this—and it was years before I even came close to that level of excellence—I had to begin with learning the rules of dance.

These training wheels of dance included line of dance (traveling around the dance floor in a counter-clockwise direction to avoid collisions and to maintain the flow of the dance), good posture (top-line, mid-line, and front-line alignment), and proper dance holds and connection with the partner (tone present in the arms and all connection points intact throughout the dance). All this before even learning dance steps and patterns! Learning these rules of dance were preparation for flowing smoothly and easily across the dance floor, just as learning the rules of life were preparation for dancing with the Divine.

Throughout my life, I've found that when learning a new skill (such as dancing, writing a book, or serving as a minister) and feeling insecure about my ability to do it right, I'd often revert to the rules—and there are always rules for everything if you're inclined to look for them. Rules would provide a structure, a beginning point, a wealth of possibilities I may not have considered. The challenge for me has always been (and continues to be) seeing the rules as guidelines or training wheels rather than rigid directives.

Even as I considered this new attitude toward rules, I still had years to grow through before I could understand that rules were a preparation for dancing with the Divine.

STEPPING OUT OF OUR COMFORT ZONES

For those of us who follow the rules and practice the shoulds of life, taking risks and stepping out of our comfort zones—valuable skills in learning to trust our inner spirit—are not on our list of priorities. Have you ever made a choice that felt exciting and totally unlike any choice you had made before and then wondered what in the world you were thinking? Following my graduation from Millersville, I was soon to learn about stepping out of my comfort zone, taking risks, and facing my fears.

Paris, Here I Come

It's June 15, 1970, and I'm in the Philadelphia International Airport waiting to board an 8:25 p.m. flight to Orly Airport in Paris where I'll meet, for the first time, my Swiss pen pal, Hans-Peter. Earlier today I wrote in my journal:

> I never thought this day would come and now it's here! I'm scared and worried and excited and nervous all at once. I'm really going abroad! Oh, my gosh!

Following the Rules

Hans-Peter and I have been writing to each other since a project in my high school English class in which we were matched with pen pals from other countries. Now he has invited me to meet him in Paris, spend time with his family in Switzerland, and then travel with him through Switzerland and Italy for three weeks.

Waiting for the plane to arrive, my heart is beating so fast I can barely breathe, my knees are shaking, and I feel a fluttery, nervous feeling in my stomach. What do I think I'm doing? Flying across the ocean by myself (I've never flown anywhere before this, and I'm afraid of heights), meeting a strange man in Paris, traveling with him for three weeks in a foreign country, and trusting him to plan the entire trip—talk about feeling out of control! Why did I think I had the courage to take a trip like this? I could still cancel my flight, have my parents drive me back home, and call Hans-Peter to tell him I won't be coming to Europe after all.

Hearing the announcement to board my flight, I take a deep breath and…

Yes, despite my fears, I hug my parents and my best friend, who tells me, "It's not every day a friend goes by herself on a trip like this," and I board the flight.

I meet Hans-Peter at the Orly airport. We spend several days in Paris taking a boat trip on the Seine River, marveling at the *Mona Lisa* at the Louvre, and viewing Paris from the top of the Eiffel Tower. We make cheese fondue while visiting Hans-Peter's family in Winterthur, Switzerland. We travel from the mountain village of Zermatt, home of the Matterhorn, to the ancient Schaffhausen

Castle and then to the serene lake town of Lugano. We ride a gondola and explore the Doge's Palace in Venice. Sometimes I feel excited, confident, and energetic, and sometimes I want to pack my bags and head for home. But I stay until the end of the planned trip.

Looking back, I'm amazed that I—a person who liked to play it safe and organize every detail ahead of time—chose to take this trip. I seemed to intuitively know that beyond my fears, the trip would open me to a new world of experiences, and so it did! Although I didn't have a name for my inner spirit yet, I was discovering a part of myself that yearned to break free of the restrictions in my life, step out of my comfort zone, and live in greater freedom and joy.

This trip was the beginning of many journeys I would take, some on my own and some with fellow travelers. Many of my trips became mind-opening experiences that would prepare me to move forward to the next phase of my life. Not only did I learn to step out of my comfort zone, but I learned to feel the fear and do it anyway—both of which would prove to be essential on my journey of dancing with the Divine.

After returning from my trip, I moved to Bel Air, Maryland, shared an apartment with a friend from college, and began teaching third grade at an elementary school in Havre de Grace, Maryland. After a year there, I moved back to Pennsylvania and for the next three years, taught third grade in the West Shore

School District. I loved teaching third graders and was very happy being a part of a supportive, caring faculty. I did, however, learn that the rule we were taught in college—"Be firm, fair, and friendly"—did not ensure that the children would sit quietly in their seats, never need to be disciplined, and do exactly what was expected of them. Another should that needed to be reevaluated!

After receiving a master's degree in education with reading certification, I changed positions at West Shore and became a reading specialist working with children in kindergarten through fifth grade, a position in which I would continue for sixteen years. I loved the freedom of being a reading specialist—working with small groups, being able to provide a variety of activities to supplement the teachers' classroom activities, and planning special schoolwide events such as "Book Character Days" when we all dressed as our favorite book characters.

A Turning Point

During these years, I was happily single until I reconnected with a man I had met at a USO dance when I was in college. Jim and I had written for several years while he was in the navy, lost touch, and reconnected several years later when, out of the blue, he wrote and asked me to marry him. We'd only spent a few weeks together at this point. The next two years were spent visiting back and forth between Pennsylvania and his home in Louisiana.

On one of his visits, while I was cooking dinner in my tiny kitchen, Jim surprised me with an engagement ring! For a romantic like me, who expected candlelight and roses, this was not the proposal I'd dreamed of. I wasn't sure I was ready or that this was the right time, but I reverted to the societal rules that still determined much of my behavior at that point. I was twenty-five years old and it was time to get married. I thought I loved him, or at least had some kind of feelings for him, so I said yes.

The ring didn't fit and we had to get it sized. Was this a sign that the marriage wouldn't fit me? However, once I had accepted Jim's proposal (I didn't know or trust my inner spirit then), I felt I had to go through with the marriage, so I proceeded. I planned and organized the wedding and created the perfect wedding on the outside, but within myself, I didn't feel the joy and excitement I expected to feel as a bride-to-be.

Not surprisingly, within a few years, the marriage was not working out as I'd hoped. Jim wanted to move back to Louisiana, and since there were many problems with his family at that time, that solution didn't feel right to me. Reluctantly, Jim agreed with my suggestion to find a marriage counselor, no doubt secretly hoping that the counselor would convince me to move to Louisiana. I hoped that the counselor would help us resolve the issues that were eroding our marriage. However, the sessions took us in an unexpected direction.

Meeting Dave

It's our first session with Dave, our thirty-something marriage counselor with a warm smile and easygoing manner. I like him immediately and feel comfortable in his presence. He asks each of us to share what is happening in our marriage. I talk about our lack of communication, my need for expressions of physical affection from Jim, and my struggle between being the perfect wife and my desire to be authentic. Jim says nothing. (He later tells me that he's sure it's obvious to Dave that I am the one instigating all the problems in our marriage.)

At the end of the session, Dave says, "The issue isn't whether or not you move to Louisiana—the issue is whether or not the marriage is worth saving."

For months, as we continued counseling, I pondered that question. I'd always believed that when I got married, it would be forever. I thought marriage would be a safe place, a place where two people would be there for each other no matter what. I was convinced that it was my responsibility to make the marriage work, and if I couldn't, I would be a failure. I struggled between following the rules and expectations I had set for myself and my marriage or admitting that I couldn't make it work and that ending the marriage might be the best solution for both of us.

When Jim and I decided to separate (he still believed the issue was going to Louisiana), I was heartbroken. I was ashamed to tell people that the marriage was over. I spent many months wondering if I could have or should have done things differently. After much soul-searching, I came to believe that we had made the right decision in ending our marriage, and I began to see the good that the counseling experience had brought to me. I learned to listen to what I wanted and needed, honor my feelings, and trust myself to make the decisions that were right for me. I felt a softening of the rules and shoulds I had imposed on myself and others. I was beginning to realize that being safe was not dependent on someone or something outside myself.

After my marriage ended, I was ready for a new beginning. Thinking I needed to make some outer changes in my life, I took several trips to California. I considered moving there and seeking a position as a book consultant for one of the book companies that produced reading series for children. During a month-long visit in California, I applied for several positions there and had three interviews, but no position opened up for me at that time. I returned home to Pennsylvania, not realizing that I was about to embark on the most exciting journey I would ever take—the journey within, the journey to discovering my inner spirit.

Chapter 3

Going Within

I'm driving my car over a 3,600-foot suspension bridge spanning the Susquehanna River, going as fast as I can to get to the other side. Suddenly I see ahead of me that the bridge ends and I'm about to drive over the edge into what appears to be vast open space. I wake up, trembling and out of breath.

This recurring dream, which I had during the time Jim and I were experiencing conflict in our marriage, led me to a dream-interpretation class at a local high school. What was this dream trying to tell me? I was convinced that the dream was warning me of a future car accident, and I didn't know what to do to prevent it. In the class, we learned that dreams are often reflections of what is going on in our lives, and as we take positive action, the issues in our dreams can be resolved.

Reluctantly, I shared my dream with the class. After several students suggested possible interpretations, the instructor asked me, "Is there some area of your life in which you're feeling out of control and overwhelmed by the situation?" My eyes opened wide and I gasped for air. That interpretation felt so right to me! How could this instructor know what my dream meant without knowing anything about me or my life situation? This dream interpretation was a catalyst to the counseling Jim and I attended, and as the instructor suggested, after I took positive action by choosing to go to counseling, I stopped having this nightmare.

TUNING IN

After my divorce, I became a member of a weekly dream-interpretation group in which we wrote down and interpreted our dreams. I began to keep a dream journal. As soon as I woke up in the morning, I'd write down anything I could remember about my dreams. I'd ask myself what part of me each character in my dream represented and what feelings and thoughts the dream evoked in me. Sometimes, before going to sleep, I'd pose a question to my dream self, and I'd find my question answered in my dream. The more I followed this process, the more I was able to interpret and understand what my dreams were telling me. Although I didn't realize it at the time, I now believe that dreams were one of the first ways my inner spirit began to speak to me.

One evening at my dream-interpretation class, we talked about our experiences with religion and spirituality. I shared that for thirty-two years, the Lutheran church had been my spiritual home. In recent years, though, I had felt that its rituals, creeds, and liturgy didn't bring me a feeling of connection with God. Attending church was an important part of my life, but I was looking for a more personal experience of knowing the presence of God. Many members of the group attended the Unity church near Harrisburg, PA. As they began to talk about it, I liked what I heard, and I decided to go to a service the following Sunday.

Have you ever been to a place for the first time and felt that you've come home? That was the feeling I had when I attended my first Unity service.

The service was nothing like what I was used to. For starters, it was held in a meeting room at a local hotel. There was no altar, pulpit, or minister dressed in a robe and stole as in the Lutheran church. Also, the service itself was much more informal—the sermon was replaced by a talk or message, the music was positive and uplifting, and there were no creeds or rote prayers. The focus was not on God "up there" but on a divine presence within us and all around us.

I thought, Wow! There are really other people who think the way I do! (I must have always been a free thinker because years later, when asked what Lutherans believed, I really didn't know. I seemed to have my own set of beliefs that I never clarified until I found Unity and discovered words to describe the beliefs that I held in my heart.)

Sometimes when we're looking for something to expand our horizons, we have no idea what we're looking for until we find it. Joining Unity coincided with my desire to go deeper within. I felt empowered by the idea of following guidance from my inner spirit, which Unity called "the Christ within." I began a new phase of my life, which was exciting but also a bit frightening, as I began to confront my old beliefs and patterns of behavior. Instead of following the shoulds of my life, I began to ask myself questions such as "What feels right for *me*?" and "What do *I* want to do?" On the one hand, I felt as though I was taking control of my life, but on the other hand, I felt out of control. I was beginning to let go of the safe and secure structures that following rules and shoulds provided and venturing into the unknown of trusting myself and my inner spirit to guide me.

At the same time as I was confronting my beliefs and behavior patterns, I was beginning to practice a meditation process I learned at Unity—going within to the silence and listening for the voice of my inner spirit. Although meditation would eventually help me become more balanced, more in touch with my feelings, and more open to inner guidance, I initially felt frustrated, uncomfortable, and skeptical. As soon as I'd attempt to "enter the silence," my mind would think of ten things that had to be done right at that very moment; ask, "How long do I have to do this?" or tell me that sitting here when I had so much to do was really a waste of time.

I persisted with the practice, starting with five to ten minutes a day, and after a few months, began to notice that I was feeling more peaceful, calm, and centered, not only during meditation but throughout my day.

During the next few years, I explored many forms of meditation, including breath meditations, chanting, centering meditations, and visualization. Through this process, I discovered that there isn't one right way to meditate, which felt wonderful to me, as I was learning to let go of rules and shoulds.

I believe that our inner spirit can lead us to the path that's right for us at any particular time. This was certainly true for me during a class I was taking at Unity Village in Lee's Summit, Missouri, in the 1990s.

A Deeper Connection with Spirit

For two hours every morning for ten days, Monday through Friday, I attended the Life of Prayer class at Unity Village. During each class, we spent one hour talking about our prayer lives, exploring different types of prayer (e.g., affirmative prayer, prayer of blessing and release, meditative prayer), developing a prayer consciousness, and feeling the presence of God throughout our daily lives. The second hour, we spent in silent meditation—yes, a whole hour in silent meditation. Our homework was to spend another hour in meditation sometime during the day. Suddenly, meditation, which had brought me a feeling of peace and calm and a deeper connection with my inner spirit, became drudgery. And yes, it began to feel like a should, something I had to do the right way.

One afternoon while attempting to practice my second hour of silent meditation and feeling discouraged by my body's desire to move and my mind's desire to chatter, I decided to take a walk. There are many lovely trails at Unity Village, and soon I was strolling along a wooded path, feeling the sun on my back and a gentle breeze blowing my hair. I took a few deep breaths, and as I walked, I began to feel lighter and more free and easy. After a few minutes of walking, I saw ahead of me a babbling brook and a bench in a secluded spot overlooking the water. I sat on the bench, breathed in and out, gazed at the sparkling water, and listened to the water flowing over the rocks and the birds singing in the background. Within a few minutes, I felt totally relaxed, at peace with myself and my world.

I sat there for what seemed like minutes, but what was, when I looked at my watch, sixty minutes—exactly the time I was asked to practice meditation. My inner spirit had led me to the perfect place where I could connect to Spirit more fully that day.

Being in nature has remained one of my favorite ways of connecting with my inner spirit and feeling more in harmony and balance with myself. We may also experience this harmony, balance, and deeper connection with our inner spirt through physical activity such as yoga, tai chi, running, sports, or dancing.

Yoga was my first experience of what is called "meditation through motion," and it helped me become more in touch with my body and be present in the moment. Since we connect with our inner spirit in the moment, thinking about the past (what we should or shouldn't have done) or living in the future (what if…, when this happens, then I will…) keeps us from hearing the voice of our inner spirit.

Developing Core Strength

We hear a lot about the value of developing physical core strength, which involves muscular tone and strength, aerobic fitness, improved condition of the heart and lungs, and enhanced posture and balance. But equally important is developing spiritual core strength, which includes perseverance, inner strength, and confidence.

While I was developing spiritual core strength through meditation, listening to my inner spirit, and examining and releasing limiting beliefs and attitudes, I was also developing physical core strength through yoga. And I found that developing one area strengthens the other: as my physical body became more balanced and flexible, so did my spiritual body.

Years later, when I began ballroom dancing, I realized that all the skills I was learning—good posture, holding the frame, controlled movement—were contributing to the development of my physical core and enabling me to perform the movements of the various styles of dance with greater flexibility, stamina, and balance.

Beyond that awareness, however, was a seeming revelation to me. One evening, after I had been taking dance lessons for about a year, I enthusiastically declared to my instructor, "Ballroom dancing is a spiritual experience!" He responded, "I think so too!" By his response, I knew he was the right instructor for me. I knew that ballroom dancing would be an opportunity for me to go deeper within myself, to discover more of who I really was, and to develop my spiritual core. It would be a means of experiencing my dance with the Divine physically, mentally, emotionally, and spiritually.

Recognizing Our Inner Spirit

Has someone ever made a suggestion that changed the course of your life? This happened to me after I'd been attending the Unity Church for about a year.

My first Unity minister, Reverend Audrey McGinnis, was a significant person and role model in my life. She had become a minister later in life, serving as a nurse and raising a family in her earlier years. I admired her positive attitude, her integrity in living the principles she taught, and her delight in seeing others grow and evolve.

One Sunday, following the service, as we were chatting over a cup of tea, Audrey confidently told me, "After you retire from teaching, you can go to Unity Village and become a Unity minister."

When had she devised this plan for my life? Why in the world would she suggest this to me? I had never indicated any interest in becoming a minister. Was it possible that she saw some of the qualities in me that I so admired in her?

Although I didn't say it out loud, I thought, "Well, there's no way I'm ever going to do that!" However, the seed was planted in my consciousness—an idea that would take almost twenty years and many experiences to come to fruition. Thinking about it now, I wonder if Spirit planted that idea in Audrey's mind to reveal to me at that very moment, knowing that if the idea had come to me directly, I would've dismissed it as nonsense.

I did become very involved in Unity of Harrisburg over the next few years. I worked on the newsletter, served on the board of directors, taught classes, and occasionally spoke at Sunday services. I also traveled to Unity Village to take continuing education courses with the intention of becoming a licensed Unity teacher.

As I became involved in Unity, I noticed a change occurring in my journaling process. Interspersed with my ramblings about various relationships in my life, I began to dialogue with my inner spirit, which at the time, I called "my higher self" or "my inner voice." I would often begin by asking a question, becoming as still as I could be, and listening for an answer, which might come immediately as an image, a thought, or a feeling. Sometimes the answer would come later as I was taking a walk, reading a book, or having a conversation with a friend. Once, I was at the bookstore at Unity Village looking for a book for a book-report assignment. I couldn't seem to find what I was looking for (I'm not sure if I *knew* what I was looking for), so I asked my inner spirit to find the book I needed to read for the report. A few minutes later, a book by Catherine Ponder fell off the shelf into my arms. "I guess that's the one," I said to myself, and when I later read the book, it was exactly what I needed to read. (I've learned that whenever I say, "That's exactly what I needed," it's a confirmation that my inner spirit is at work.)

Our inner spirit speaks to us all the time, but we have to be aware of it. We have to create the time and the space—the inner quiet—so we can hear our inner spirit's voice. *A Course in Miracles*, a channeled book of wisdom, states, "Spirit speaks only as loud as our willingness to listen." Our inner spirit may speak to us mentally, through persistent thoughts or images; emotionally, through our feelings of excitement, peace, joy, calm, or certainty; or kinesthetically, through physical sensations such as a pain in the neck, chills, feeling comfortable or uncomfortable in our bodies, or feeling the energy of a place or person.

The more we take time to listen to and notice these signs, the more we learn to recognize the voice of our inner spirit. As we begin to follow the guidance of our inner spirit, we experience greater peace of mind; increased energy, creativity, and clarity; a sense of purpose and direction; and a feeling of being in the flow of life.

As I continued my journey of going within, following this inner voice was becoming more and more important to me. During this time, I wrote in my journal:

> The commitment I need to make now is to follow my inner voice completely. That is the only commitment I need to make, and that is everything!

Have you ever made a commitment without knowing exactly what you were committing to? I had no idea when I made this commitment that choosing to follow my inner spirit would, in time, lead me to step way out of my comfort zone and to make choices that I never dreamed I would make.

Going Within

WHOLE BRAIN LEARNING THEORY

One of the choices I made during my years as a reading specialist at the West Shore School District was to study Whole Brain Learning Theory, a concept that became popular in the 1980s. In Whole Brain Learning Theory, each part of the brain is associated with a different function and ability. The left side of the brain is associated with logical, sequential, reality-based thinking and following directions. The right side of the brain is associated with intuitive, creative thinking, art expression, and physical movement.

I became fascinated with the differences between left-brain and right-brain learning. When I began to practice meditation, I realized I wasn't using my intuitive, right-brain side as often as my logical, rational, left-brain side. I felt that developing the right side of my brain would help me move out of my head and into my heart. Along with my spiritual practices of deep breathing, meditation, and yoga, I began to do exercises using visualization, music, color, and art, which helped me get more in touch with my intuitive side. One of the greatest shifts I experienced was through a process called upside-down drawing, from the book *Drawing on the Right Side of the Brain* by Betty Edwards.

One rainy Saturday afternoon, I turned to page fifty-two in my book, where I found an inverted picture—"Portrait of Igor Stravinsky" by Picasso—and instructions on how to draw this picture upside down. This process was to allow my left brain to relax for a while and allow my right brain to take over. I would be copying the upside-down image, and when I finished, my picture would supposedly look like the one I was copying. ("Oh, sure," I thought. "My picture will never look like that. I'm the one whose art projects never looked like the teacher's model.")

I looked at the drawing. I looked at the angles and shapes and lines. And I began at the top of the drawing, copying each line, moving from line to line, putting it all together like a jigsaw puzzle. I resisted the temptation to name the parts as I was drawing (a left-brain skill) and simply focused on lines, curves, and how they fit together in space (a right-brain skill). If I thought too much about what I was doing or tried to figure it out, I lost focus. At some point in the process, I began to shift from "I can't do this" to "I am doing this." I became lost in the lines and spaces. I had shifted from my left brain to my right brain to complete the task.

About an hour later, I finished the drawing, turned it right side up, and guess what—it looked like the picture I was copying! My right brain, the hemisphere appropriate for the task of drawing, had taken over and completed the task.

So, did this experiment transform me into an artist? No, definitely not. I didn't find the experience particularly easy or enjoyable. But what I did learn is that through turning a picture upside down, looking at it differently, and then drawing from that perspective, I could do something I was told I couldn't do: draw a picture that looked almost exactly like the original. Had I tried to draw the picture the way I'd been taught in school, I wouldn't have known how to start. Not only had I learned the importance of shifting my perspective artistically but also of shifting my belief system from "I can't do it" to "Yes, I can."

Have you ever noticed that when we change our perspective, our life changes? This valuable lesson in changing perspective was to make quite a difference in my life in ways I couldn't yet imagine.

Learning to Follow Our Inner Spirit

The more we tune in to our inner spirit, the more we receive inner nudges—gentle suggestions or proddings to take a step forward, often a step out of our comfort zone.

One day while I was using some of the whole-brain techniques with my reading-challenged students, I felt an inner nudge to take a one-year sabbatical from teaching to visit and study in places where whole-brain learning was practiced.

After working in the school district for fifteen years, I was long overdue to take a sabbatical. During a sabbatical I would receive half my salary during that year and would promise to return to my position for at least a year to share what I had learned during that time. I'd never taken advantage of this opportunity in the past, partly because I didn't think I could live on half my salary for a year. But with my new belief based on the prosperity teachings I'd learned at Unity—that if I followed what I was guided to do, the money, resources, and everything I'd need would be provided— I decided to trust my inner spirit and step out of my comfort zone: I took a yearlong sabbatical to further study whole-brain learning, visualization, and meditation in educational settings.

During my sabbatical journey, not only did I observe and discover new whole-brain techniques to use personally and with my students, but the year of travel and study confirmed my newly held belief that for every outer journey, there is a corresponding inner journey. These words, written in the introduction to my sabbatical photo album express my excitement at this awareness:

> This book is a remembrance of some of the places and events that were part of my sabbatical journey this past year. There can, however, be no outer journey without a corresponding inner journey. The changes that took place within me—the growth, the letting go, the surrendering to what is, learning to live with, and yes, even enjoy, uncertainty; seeing possibilities; seeking to find and express wholeness in my life—that's been the real heart of my journey, and that's what I will always remember!

Have you ever heard of the concept of unstructured time? Unstructured time is a right-brain way of living that involves letting go of a rigid schedule and allowing time to follow the energy of the moment—to make choices in the moment instead of planning out our day ahead of time. This idea of unstructured time, which I became aware of during my sabbatical, can be very helpful in our dance with the Divine, as we learn to listen to the leading of our inner spirit. It helped me to enjoy greater freedom in my life, to feel more in the divine flow.

DIVINE DISCONTENT

Returning home from my sabbatical, I was looking forward to applying what I had learned with the children in my classes at West Shore School District but was also feeling that my time at West Shore was coming to an end. I was experiencing what Mary Manin Morrissey describes (in her book *Building Your Field of Dreams*) as "divine discontent," the feeling of restlessness and the desire to step into new possibilities. But I didn't yet know what those new possibilities were—or the challenges that this next year would bring.

Sometimes when it's time for us to make a change in our lives and we hesitate, our life (most likely our inner spirit, which opts for growth and expansion rather than staying safe and in a rut) presents challenges that push us to make the decisions we need to make. The first challenge in my life in the year following my sabbatical was a teachers' strike, and the second was the mother of one of my students.

If you've ever been involved in a strike, you know that tempers can flare as each side believes they are right and the other side is wrong. Although I had embraced this "us vs. them" idea fifteen years earlier when a strike appeared imminent, this time I couldn't identify with the teachers' feeling of lack of respect from the administrators and the belief that we were on different sides. Weren't we all there to provide the best possible education for the students?

When the strike vote occurred, it was approved by over 95% of the teachers. Because it didn't feel right to me, I voted against it.

Pressure was intense to join the picket line and to refuse to cross it to go to work when the schools were open. I struggled with following the expectations of my colleagues vs. following what felt right for me (and what I believed to be the guidance of my inner spirit). What did I do? I didn't join a picket line, but I also didn't cross it. I took one step in the direction of following my inner spirit and one step—although I'd rather not admit it—to appease my fellow teachers.

What I learned then is how difficult it can be to follow our inner truth when it's not the view of the majority of others in our life. And what I've learned since then is that no matter how much we learn to trust and follow our inner spirit, we'll have times when, because of fear or doubt, we fall short of our own expectations. As my inner spirit often reminds me, *"It's okay. We're all in the process of growing and unfolding."*

My second challenge of the year following my sabbatical occurred when we returned to school after the strike. Outwardly, the strike issues appeared to be resolved, but I could feel the resentment and lack of trust that still existed among teachers, parents of students, and administrators. Into that atmosphere, I began my pilot program, approved by the West Shore administration and based on my studies during my sabbatical year. In the program, we would use whole-brain techniques such as visualization and imagery for increasing reading skills in the second-grade classes at the elementary school in which I was serving as a reading specialist. I used similar techniques in my work with children in the special reading program, and I taught the skills to other teachers and administrators in the district. I led a voluntary visualization group for teachers before classes began in the morning. I was finding the techniques to work well with children in my classes, the second-grade teachers were reporting positive feedback, and the teachers who attended the morning visualization group appeared to be more relaxed and centered as they moved through their day.

However, this accepting atmosphere was to be short-lived. Enter the mother of a child in the second-grade program who objected to the visualizations we were using, calling them brainwashing. She asked to have her child removed from the class when these activities took place. Over the course of the next few months, this mother gathered a small group of parents, contacted a lawyer, and continued to push for elimination of the pilot program. I often found her standing outside my classroom, scowling and taking notes on the activities I was using with the children.

The administration supported me until the conflict became too intense, especially with issues from the strike not fully resolved, and then decided to drop the pilot program. I was encouraged to keep doing what I was doing in my classes with special reading; in other words, doing it quietly and unobtrusively. I was beginning to wonder if these roadblocks were signs from my inner spirit that it was time for me to leave the West Shore School District.

A Leap of Faith

During that year, the feeling deep within me that there was something else I was meant to do grew stronger and more persistent. My inner spirit seemed to be telling me that it was time to leave, even though I didn't know what I was going to do next. Leave a secure position with a good salary and health benefits without knowing what I would do next? Although I'd learned to trust the voice of my inner spirit more and more over the past few years, this idea seemed irresponsible. I was a person who planned ahead and didn't take a step until I knew where I was going.

The voice of my inner spirit grew stronger in the next months. The conflict within me got more intense as well. As I tried to ignore the promptings of my inner spirit, I grew increasingly frustrated with myself and the work I was doing. I also began to experience debilitating headaches and pain in my shoulders and back. During that time I wrote in my journal:

> I have a strong feeling that I'm to resign from the West Shore School District without knowing what I'm to do next. This could be the most illogical thing I have ever done. My heart reminds me of the words of my hero, Ray Kinsella from the movie *Field of Dreams*: "Until I heard the voice, I'd never done a crazy thing in my whole life." It is an idea that, though frightening, feels joyful and freeing to me. But do I have the courage? That's the question.

Unlike Ray Kinsella, my inner spirit wasn't telling me to plow under my field of crops and build a baseball field, but the idea of leaving my job of eighteen years felt just as illogical to me.

For months, my spiritual counselor had been encouraging me to listen to my inner spirit and take a step in the direction I was being guided toward. Was this what it meant to commit to following my inner spirit—following its guidance no matter how illogical it seemed? Somehow, I knew this was a turning point in my life. Would I choose to play it safe and stay where I was even though I knew it was no longer where I was meant to be, or would I take a giant leap of faith and trust that my inner spirit would guide me through all the changes I knew were ahead of me?

Finally, after a year of struggling to make the choice—*should I stay or should I go?*—the moment of decision arrived. One evening in mid-September 1989, I was taking my usual evening walk around my neighborhood when, in the silence of my being, I clearly heard: "*You are to leave at the end of December. It will be a Christmas gift to yourself.*" I knew at that moment it was the decision I had to make, and I was finally ready to take that step.

When I look back at this moment, it's as if my inner spirit was saying, *"Come dance with me. Trust me to lead you in this dance of your life."*

And in that moment, I said yes, not only to leaving my teaching position of eighteen years—which was in itself a huge leap of faith—but to trusting my inner spirit to lead me in my dance with the Divine, no matter where that dance was to take me.

Chapter 4

Moving Through Transition

Have you ever felt like you were in a small boat in the middle of the ocean—you didn't know where you were and nothing seemed familiar to you? You felt abandoned and alone, and you wondered if you'd ever be on firm ground again. You were terrified that at any minute you could sink in the middle of the vast sea and be lost forever.

These are common feelings when we're experiencing a transition—a major change that encompasses many parts of our life and requires extensive adjustment in our lifestyle, values, and identity. A transition may be triggered by an illness, a loss of a relationship, a death, a change of job or location, or inner growth. Each transition consists of three stages: an ending, a void, and a new beginning. If you're feeling lost and alone, unsure of where you are and what your next steps will be, you're in the void.

Adrift in the void is where I found myself on January 2, 1990, when I left my eighteen-year teaching career and began my life as a self-employed person. Compounded by the fact that I didn't know what I was going to be doing career-wise, I had to learn a new way of life that challenged my belief system. I no longer had to get up at 6:00 a.m. to get ready for work each morning. I no longer had a paycheck coming in every two weeks. I had lots of time on my hands and wasn't sure what to do with it.

On the first day after Christmas vacation—when I would have returned to the West Shore School District had I continued my employment there—I wrote in my journal:

> Today I wake up and lie in bed on this first day of my self-employment. What do I feel? A mixture of excitement, freedom, apprehension, doubt. What do I do first? Have I really left my teaching position without knowing what I will do next? What will the first year of this next phase of my life bring?

Many times over the coming years I'd wonder what in the world I'd been thinking, leaving behind all that was familiar and secure to me. I was undertaking a journey not only to find the work that was mine to do in the world but to determine whether the spiritual principles I'd learned really did work. Could I really trust that whatever I needed—money, time, resources—would be there for me if I listened to and followed my inner spirit?

The truth is that spiritual principles are always working, but when we become aware of them and consciously choose to align with them—as I did when I left my teaching position and chose to say yes to trusting my inner spirit to guide me in my dance with the Divine—we begin to step out into the world differently. I'd been learning to recognize, listen to, and follow my inner spirit for about eight years, but living what I'd learned in every aspect of my life sometimes felt like being in that small boat in the middle of the ocean—lost and alone in the void.

Navigating the Void

In a time of transition, the void is usually the most difficult part. There is no sense of movement. We often feel empty and alone. Our fears of abandonment, helplessness, and hopelessness are triggered. The question we most ask in the void is, "When will this be over?"

Over time, I've learned that the void stage of a transition does have benefits for us, especially in the area of our spiritual growth. In Eastern religions, the void is considered "sacred emptiness," a state of knowing our true nature. The void gives us time to become clear about what we need/want and who we really are. Because it's a time when the old rules and beliefs no longer work, it's the perfect time to tune in and listen to our inner spirit. And, as I was told by my inner spirit when I began this phase of my life, *"Your work right now is your spiritual growth. Your work is learning to trust your inner spirit in each decision you make."*

During this period of seeking to understand myself and the changes that were occurring in my life, my journal became my constant companion. I continued the process of dialoguing with my inner spirit that I'd begun several years earlier—asking questions, listening for answers, and following the suggestions I was given. I also began setting intentions as part of my journaling process. I was learning that intentions could be statements of what I wanted to attract and call into my life and/or guiding principles for how I wanted to live—a way to bring my heart and mind into alignment. I began to set intentions for the day (for instance, to be a peaceful presence that day or to notice all the blessings of the day) as well as for the week, month, and year. Unlike goals, which I often created with my mind and then set specific steps to take in order to reach, intentions seemed to come from my heart, guided by my inner spirit, and often came about in totally unexpected ways.

One of my first intentions, which I wrote at the beginning of a new year, was to speak at a Unity Sunday service. At the time, I thought, "Where did that come from?" I hadn't been consciously thinking about it. In fact, I thought, "Why would anyone ask me to speak at a Unity service?" (I'd only been attending for about a year and felt I had lots to learn before I'd be qualified to speak.) Several weeks later, the minister at Unity, Audrey McGinnis, called and asked me to speak when she was on vacation. That was the first of many intentions I set that would, without my trying to create the results I wanted, manifest in exactly the right time and in the right way.

Moving Through Transition

I highly recommend asking questions or setting intentions as part of your journaling process in a time of transition in your life. When we're feeling lost and alone, who but our inner spirit can know what's best for us and guide us to follow our own unique dance with the Divine?

In a transitional period in our lives when we're learning new skills and developing new beliefs, we often feel uncomfortable and unsure of ourselves. I experienced this firsthand years later when I began ballroom dancing. During that time, I became aware of a transitional period from learning to follow the basic rules and steps to feeling as though I was really dancing to the music with joy and ease—a process that mirrored my dance with the Divine. It gave new meaning to transitioning from one phase of life to another.

In dancing, I found that when I was introduced to a new move—especially one that required intricate steps, graceful arm movements, and perfect timing to coordinate it all—I felt awkward or self-conscious at first, definitely not ready to try it on a crowded dance floor.

As I continued to practice, I would move to what I call a conscious phase. In this phase, I could do the step and coordinate the movements more efficiently and easily but still had to think it through when I performed it. After a time of continuing to use and practice the step or skill, it would become more natural to me and I'd feel more comfortable and at ease. At this point, I'd be ready to use the step or skill at a social dance or party.

Like the process of learning new steps in ballroom dancing, when I was learning to follow my inner spirit and test my new beliefs and attitudes, I began with discomfort and lack of trust in my inner spirit's guidance, hesitating to take the steps I was guided to take. I then moved to consciously taking steps as guided and observing how I felt and what results occurred. Over the years, I learned to listen, take steps as guided with greater confidence and ease, and enjoy the feeling of dancing with the Divine that following my inner spirit brought me. This transitional time in my life was definitely preparation for learning to dance with the Divine more joyfully and gracefully.

Trusting God as Source

The first year of my new life led me to private tutoring for children with reading challenges, creating self-esteem groups for children and adults, facilitating whole-brain learning workshops and seminars, and spending a great deal of time worrying about where the money would come from to cover my bills and the necessities of life. Because I anticipated that I wouldn't have money coming in at first, I had withdrawn funds from my retirement account to pay my living expenses until I became self-sufficient. How quickly those funds disappeared, and how often I found that meeting my expenses was challenging without a regular income to count on!

One of the most powerful prosperity teachings I learned when I began attending Unity Church was the principle of trusting God as my source. It wasn't until I left my teaching position that I learned what this meant. To be perfectly honest, I think I had seen the West Shore School District, my employer for eighteen years, as my source. After all, I received a check every two weeks, my health benefits were paid for, and I felt comfortable financially.

Fortunately, two years after I left my teaching position, I took a class at Unity Village on Metaphysical Bible Teaching, a method of viewing the Bible symbolically and applying it to our own life experiences, which would help me understand what trusting God as my source meant.

One day, we were studying the story of the Israelites leaving Egypt and the bondage of slavery and then wandering for forty years in the wilderness. Each day, the Israelites were given just enough manna (a bread-like substance) for that day and were instructed to trust that every day they would be provided exactly what they needed for that day. Sounds easy, right? Not so much. Some days they were afraid and tried to hoard the manna (just in case it didn't arrive the next day), but the manna would spoil after one day. Sometimes they became angry and afraid and screamed at Moses, "Why did you bring us on this journey? We were better off in Egypt, even though we were not free." (I suspect that most of us, if we were to undertake this journey, would have similar doubts and fears.)

Sometimes, although we've heard a story many times, we hear it in a new way. This time when I heard the story of the Israelites wandering in the wilderness, I knew that within that story was a message just for me. I began to apply this principle of trusting

God as my source in my life. Whenever I became fearful about my finances or wondered if I had enough money to pay an upcoming bill, I would pause, take time in silence, and hear my inner spirit ask, *"Do you have enough for today?"* Amazingly, the answer was always yes. When I needed money, it was always there. Beyond that, I heard, *"Do not be afraid to use what you have. When what you have is gone, more will come."* (Just like the manna in the wilderness.) And somehow, more always did come. This happened in a variety of ways: I'd be invited to speak or to present a workshop, someone who had borrowed money from me would suddenly repay me, or I'd be inspired with a divine idea—an idea for a next step clearly guided by my inner spirit.

One of these divine ideas was to form my own business, which I felt clearly guided to call Integrity. To me, *integrity* meant following my inner spirit and was a reminder that when I acted from integrity, my life flowed. When my life didn't flow, I needed to go within and discern where I wasn't in harmony with my inner spirit. (What a clever way my inner spirit had to remind me of my commitment to follow my inner spirit—through the name of my new business venture.)

Through my new business, I began facilitating personal-growth workshops and seminars, leading support groups, and doing inspirational speaking at Unity churches and other venues.

Have you ever heard the statement (created by Richard Bach in his book *Illusions*) "You teach best what you most need to learn"? Workshops I created and facilitated—Life Transitions, Facing Your Fears, Trusting Your Inner Spirit, Finding Inner Peace, and Living

Your Purpose—were based on lessons I was learning and tools that were helping me navigate a new way of living. As I facilitated these workshops, I discovered that I wasn't the only one who needed the tools I was offering. I was delighted to find that students in my classes also found the teachings helpful in learning to live a more peaceful, joy-filled, purposeful life.

SECOND-GUESSING

Although I was becoming more and more comfortable with recognizing and following my inner spirit, I would often second-guess myself. Was I really following my inner spirit, especially when things didn't turn out as I had expected? I was discovering that it's often easier and more comfortable to follow rules, which are the same in all situations, than to go within, listen, and do what feels right in the moment.

In the early stages of learning to trust and follow my inner spirit, I would feel clearly guided to take a specific step, then two hours later, I'd think, "What have I done? I should have…" or "I shouldn't have…" and I'd be plagued by self-doubt. Sometimes the fear of making a mistake would keep me from taking the step I was guided to take.

Over the years, I learned that we can't give up if we make mistakes (and I made plenty in those early years, mostly following the shoulds and shouldn'ts). I also learned that mistakes are not errors in judgment but guideposts to lessons that we need to learn in order to live a more flowing, harmonious life.

At one point when I was doubting myself and wondering if I'd have enough money to pay upcoming bills, I received a call from the West Shore School District. They were having difficulty finding someone to fill a six-month position for a reading specialist and urged me to accept the position. How tempting it was to accept the position and not have to worry about money for six months! Although I felt that this wasn't the right choice for me, I almost let my fears move me to accept. In the early days of following my inner spirit, if I was feeling unsure of what path to take, I'd sometimes ask for a sign. So that's what I chose to do. Within a few days, I received a call to present my Positive Imaging workshop at a local school district. What a made-to-order sign it was! Just as I was focusing on a more positive vision for my life than returning to the position I'd outgrown, I was invited to present a workshop on how to envision and manifest our dreams and desires. I knew this was an opportunity to move forward rather than going back. I declined the position at West Shore. In the battle between following my fear or my inner spirit, my inner spirit won. (At least *this* time!)

Although I didn't think too much about this choice at the time, looking back, I see it as another turning point in my life. Before leaving West Shore, I was sure my security came from my tenured position. Now I was becoming aware that my security came from trusting myself and my inner spirit.

THE NEXT STEP

Sometimes our inner spirit is waiting for just the right time to lead us to a step that will be the beginning of a whole new way of life for us.

In 1991 I was asked by my minister at the Unity Church to begin a Unity study group, and I accepted. Ten of us began meeting at a State Farm insurance office conference room two Sunday evenings a month, and I would choose each meeting's discussion topic, such as Prayer and Meditation, Positive Thinking, or Divine Guidance. Starting this group and wanting to learn more about the topics we were discussing inspired me to return to Unity Village for a week or two at a time for several years and eventually, in 1994, to become a licensed Unity teacher. I had now taken a step on the path to ministry that Audrey McGinnis, my first Unity minister, had suggested to me over ten years earlier. Although becoming a minister was still a long way in the future, the idea had begun to take shape in my mind and heart. In 1991 I wrote in my journal:

> I had a vision today of my possible future, at least that is what I think it was. While driving to our Unity study group this morning, I saw myself as a minister. I was filled with joy and a sense of knowing this was what I was meant to do. Of course, it was so obvious! As my head gave each reason why I couldn't do it, an answer appeared for how I could. I felt as though I was looking ahead to where I was going. I wasn't ready to take the steps

to get me there yet. Maybe it wasn't the right time; maybe I had some growing to do. In this feeling of communion with the me I am going to be, I said, "I am willing to serve in whatever way I am meant to serve."

Then I came back to present time and put aside this vision until the right time, ten years later. (I know now that my inner spirit was going to keep giving me divine nudges until I said yes to this calling.)

SYNCHRONICITIES

Sometimes it isn't until later, when we look back upon the timing of events in our lives, that we see events' synchronicities (a term that Carl Jung defined as "meaningful coincidences").

In 1991, when I began the Unity study group, I also became involved in ballroom dancing, as a National Ballroom Dance Association group was starting in the Harrisburg area. I was so interested in dancing at the time (having dabbled in it a few years earlier) that I decided to move our study group from Sunday evenings to Sunday mornings so that I could attend the dances. This proved to be a wise decision, as it established the pattern of our having regular meetings on Sunday mornings and was a step toward becoming a ministry rather than a study group. Little did I know that the lessons I would learn in ballroom dancing over the years to come would mirror my spiritual journey, help me integrate the lessons into my physical body, and be the subject for this book.

In 1994 our Unity study group moved to a new location—a Best Western Inn in Hershey, Pennsylvania—where we held Sunday services for six years. (We also held classes during the week at the Hershey Library.) During this time, I experienced more synchronicities, which I now recognize as signs of being in the divine flow, following the guidance of inner spirit.

For instance, the room at the Best Western was pleasant—it had space for about fifty people, a small area where we could have refreshments after the service, and a big picture window in the back, which allowed in lots of sunshine—but we had no keyboard in the room and no one to provide music for congregational singing. This problem was soon remedied, however, when I "coincidentally" met a woman in a nearby bookstore called The Inner Connection. She had been searching for a Unity church in the area and offered to accompany us on her accordion. Although accordion music was not my preferred choice for a Sunday service, this option provided accompaniment for singing songs, and eventually we acquired a small keyboard and a new musician to play it.

We also needed a treasurer to oversee the finances of our group, but no one in the group wanted the position or felt they had the skills to serve in this way. However, after one of the services, a woman attending for the first time told me how much she enjoyed being there and asked if there was something she could do to help. Not daring to hope for a positive response, I tentatively replied, "Well, we are looking for a treasurer. Do you have any experience in that area?"

"I'd love to serve as treasurer," she said. "I've served as a treasurer for several different groups, and it's something I thoroughly enjoy."

Never doubt the power of Spirit to find the perfect people at the right time in the right way!

During this time of transition in my life, I felt as though I had two part-time ministries—the Unity group and Integrity—and I believed that at some point, one of them would become my full-time work.

During one of my week-long sessions at Unity Village, as I was sharing my journey of the last few years—teaching, serving as a reading specialist, leading workshops and seminars, speaking at churches, starting my own business—a fellow student said to me, "It seems to me that all your experiences have been preparing you for ministry." A perfectly logical conclusion, and this time, I was ready to take the next step to becoming an ordained Unity minister.

In July 2000 I applied to the Association of Unity Churches Field Licensing Program, a four-year program designed for those who are licensed as Unity teachers and are serving as spiritual leaders of a ministry. If I was accepted in this program, I would study at Unity Village once a year and have a mentor who'd oversee a program of self-study and reflection while I continued to serve as spiritual leader at my local ministry.

CHURCH FOR FREE

At the same time, our group was becoming frustrated with conditions at the Best Western: often our room was not cleaned or set up when we'd arrive for our Sunday services, there was no space for Sunday school for the children, and the rent was being raised beyond what we were willing to pay. So we began searching for a church building where we could grow and expand our ministry—ideally, a location with space for an office and Sunday school, a fellowship area, and a larger meeting room for Sunday services. We looked everywhere, from a log cabin to a Masonic lodge, but nothing felt right or was affordable for our small core group of twenty-five to thirty people.

In Unity, we practice the spiritual principle of blessing and releasing to make room for greater good. At one Sunday service in August 2000, I led a prayer of blessing in which I expressed gratitude for the room in which we'd been meeting for six years, for the friendships we'd made there, and for the opportunity to begin our ministry. I then released the space to whomever would be using it next and affirmed that we would find the perfect place for our new church home.

A week later, I was reading the *Sunday Patriot News* want ads (something I never looked at but somehow felt guided to do on that day) and found this ad: "Church building for free!" Thinking it was a joke, I called the number listed in the paper and discovered that a local builder and developer had bought an existing church building in Palmyra, Pennsylvania (just ten minutes from where we were currently meeting) and wanted to donate it to a qualified church. Since we had incorporated as a church the month before, we were eligible. In September 2000, after a series of meetings with the builder and developer, we were chosen to be the recipients of this incredible gift! Who would ever have thought that my inner spirit would find our congregation a church through the want ads of the Sunday newspaper? Can you imagine the excitement we felt at having our very own church with a spacious sanctuary seating up to 150 people and encircled by exquisite stained-glass windows, plus rooms for fellowship, classes, youth education, an office—everything we'd envisioned for our new church home…for free? *That* we had never imagined.

What else I hadn't imagined was the fear I felt as this new phase of life was opening up for me and my congregation. Though we expected to grow in numbers now that we had a permanent location and space to develop our ministry, would we be able to manage a hundred-year-old building that would doubtlessly need renovation and extensive maintenance over the years? Was this the right place for us at this time? What would be expected of me as spiritual leader of this new ministry? Would I be accepted into the field-licensing program leading to ordination as a Unity minister?

I spent hours in the silence asking questions and listening to the voice of my inner spirit. The message I received was this:

> *Since leaving your teaching position, you've known that you've been in a time of transition. It is now time to move from the void to a new beginning, to the next phase of your life. All the*

pieces are coming together for you and for your congregation. Trust the process.

I knew that fear was not uncommon when moving out of the void to a new beginning. It was time once again to step out of my comfort zone and trust that if we'd been led to this free church (and I believe that we had been), whatever we needed—money, resources, courage—would be provided. I also knew that when we set an intention to grow and have the courage to take the steps we're guided to take, no matter how unusual those steps may seem, miracles occur.

My inner spirit was right. All the pieces for a new beginning were coming together for me and my congregation. We had released our meeting room at the Best Western Inn, received the amazing gift of a free church, found a new and larger temporary space in a nearby Comfort Inn where we would meet until we could move into our new church home, and were beginning to plan our move to Palmyra in April. Only one piece was missing: my acceptance into the field-licensing program.

The day after Thanksgiving 2000, two months after receiving the gift of our new church, I received an invitation to come to Unity Village the following March for an interview for the field-licensing program.

KNOWING FOR SURE

In March 2001, I arrived at Unity Village feeling very nervous and unsure of myself. While I was walking along the pathway through the village, trying to drink in the beauty of the Mediterranean-style architecture and the majestic fountains I so loved, I met several ministerial students from the second-year class. They invited me to join them for dinner and welcomed me into their group. I had often heard of soul groups—people we feel we've known forever, with whom our soul resonates physically, mentally, emotionally, and spiritually—but I'd never felt this connection so strongly before. I immediately felt welcomed, loved, and accepted. It was as if they were saying to me, "We're so glad you're here. We've been waiting for you to come." When I expressed concerns for my interviews the following day, they assured me, "Of course you'll be accepted into the field-licensing program."

In the next few days, I had interviews with directors of the program, a psychologist, and a psychiatrist; took a written test; and presented a message and meditation for review by several ministers. Through it all, I felt supported by my soul group. Field-licensing classes are always small, but that year I was one of only three applicants. At the end of the week, I was accepted into the program, the only one to be accepted that year. When I was told I was on the way to becoming a Unity minister, I burst into tears. Those who evaluated me said, "Surely you knew you would be accepted, didn't you?" I had known I was meant to be there, but once again, I had doubted. When I returned home and shared with my congregation the news that I'd been accepted into the program, they said, "We all knew you would be." Even though I felt my inner spirit guiding me all the way, it seems everyone knew for sure but me!

In April 2001 my inner spirit had words of confirmation for me as I began this new experience in my life:

> *Your ministry began a long time ago when you entered this earth plane (no, even before that) and took a quantum leap in consciousness when you left your life as a teacher in the West Shore School District and ventured out on your own. Now, in choosing to enter the field-licensing program to become an ordained Unity minister and entering into full-time ministry, another phase of your ministry is beginning. And yes, you have within you everything you need. You will grow and unfold in the process.*

Once again, my inner spirit knew exactly what I needed to hear as I entered this path to becoming an ordained Unity minister.

NEW BEGINNING

Have you ever noticed that just when life seems to be flowing easily and effortlessly, an unexpected obstacle appears on your pathway? When I returned from Unity Village, we discovered that our church building's previous owners had experienced a delay in completing their new church home and would not be able to vacate until April 10. This meant that in order to hold our first service in our new home on Easter Sunday, April 15, we would have only five days to move in, install our sound system, prepare the sanctuary for our first service, and organize a reception following the service.

This time, instead of focusing on the obstacle, I trusted that we would have all the time we required to do what needed to be done. With much help from our congregation and friends, we were able to complete the tasks in time.

What a joyful experience to celebrate Easter Sunday and our new beginning in our new church home at 39 East Main Street in Palmyra, Pennsylvania! When I stood behind my pulpit for the first time, I felt a sense of belonging. In this place, in this moment, I knew that I was exactly where I was meant to be, where my inner spirit had patiently led me through the ups and downs, the doubts, and the fears of my eleven-year transition from leaving West Shore. I was ready for new opportunities, new commitments, new challenges. I was ready for a new beginning as minister of Unity of Palmyra. I had learned, and would continue to learn, the importance of following my inner spirit, trusting in perfect divine timing, and taking the steps I was guided to take.

Four years later, after completing the field-licensing program, I was ordained at my church in the presence of my congregation, family, and friends. It was the day I would experience the joining together of my spiritual journey and my love for ballroom dancing in a beautiful dance with the Divine.

Part Three

Dance Lessons

*Dancing is like life. The lessons of one
are the lessons of another.*

– Savion Glover

In March 1995, I attended a memorial service for my friend Jim, a fellow ballroom dancer. Jim's obituary noted his membership in the two organizations that were most important to him: Christ Lutheran Church and the United States Amateur Ballroom Dance Association. Honoring Jim's love for his church and for ballroom dancing, the minister's eulogy compared life to a dance. The words touched me deeply and confirmed my belief in the connection between life, spirituality, and dance.

Following this service and after I'd been taking private dance lessons for about a year, I noticed that many of the lessons I was learning in ballroom dancing mirrored lessons I was learning on my spiritual journey following my inner spirit. As I was learning to dance in harmony with a ballroom dance partner, I was discovering how to dance a more flowing, joyful, peace-filled dance with the Divine.

In this section of my book, it's my delight to share the ballroom dance lessons that helped me integrate spiritual lessons into my life. At the end of each chapter are "dance steps" to assist you in applying these lessons to your unique dance with the Divine. May your dance be filled with peace, joy, and love!

Chapter 5

Leading and Following

Looking back at an entry in my journal from 1992, I found:

> I've always been good at leading. Maybe dancing is the most important thing I can do to learn to follow with ease and even with joy!

I began ballroom dancing at a time when I was learning to let God lead in my daily life. I was in a time of transition. After leaving my eighteen-year teaching position in the West Shore School District, I was exploring my options for what I was going to do with the rest of my life. I was also ending an on-again, off-again three-year relationship that seemed to consist of more struggle and conflict than joy. I was beginning to see that my efforts to control my life weren't bringing me the peace and harmony I longed to experience. At the same time, I was discovering in ballroom dancing that leading and following are essential to the flow of the dance. Maybe it was time for me to explore what it meant to let go and let God lead in my daily life.

Have you ever received a message through a book, an inspirational talk, or a conversation with a friend that was exactly what you needed to hear at that time in your life? I once received such a message about letting go and letting God lead. The message arrived on a cold, wintry January morning when I was sitting at my computer, checking my emails, watching the snow fall outside my window, and longing for some words of inspiration to brighten my day.

As I was glancing through the multitude of emails I'd received, one particular subject line caught my attention: "Dancing with God." Curious, I opened the email and read these words:

> When I meditated on the word *guidance*, I kept seeing *dance* at the end of the word. I remember reading that doing God's will is a lot like dancing. When two people try to lead, nothing feels right. The movement doesn't flow with the music, and everything is quite uncomfortable and jerky. When one person realizes that and lets the other lead, both bodies begin to flow with the music. One gives gentle cues, perhaps with a nudge to the back or by pressing lightly in one direction or another. It's as if two become one body, moving beautifully. The dance takes surrender, willingness, and attentiveness from one person, and gentle guidance and skill from the other.

Leading and Following

> My eyes drew back to the word *guidance*. When I saw *G*, I thought of God, followed by *u* and *I dance*. God, you and I dance. As I lowered my head, I became willing to trust that I would get guidance about my life. Once again, I became willing to let God lead.
>
> – Jean Rhodes

Aha! Jean Rhodes had clarified the connection I was feeling between ballroom dancing and my dance with God. Now I had words to guide me as I explored the spiritual lessons I was learning in ballroom dancing.

When we dance with the Divine by following our divine guidance, our inner spirit gently leads us. If we follow rather than resist, we begin to see a beautiful harmony and flow of life in our daily experiences. But how do we recognize divine guidance? Unlike the gentle nudge to the back in ballroom dancing, divine guidance comes from within—as an inner nudge that gently speaks to us in the silence of our being. This inner prompting may guide us to take that trip we've always wanted to take, write that book we've been wanting to write for years, call that friend we haven't heard from in a very long time but who's often been in our thoughts in recent days. It may be leading us to make a significant life change—to leave a job that no longer feels satisfying, even though it's financially profitable, or to leave a relationship that's no longer loving and supportive. Although the inner promptings may seem difficult to follow, they can—and usually do—lead to greater fulfillment in our lives, greater self-expression, or a greater sense of purpose and meaning.

The guidance we receive is designed especially for each one of us for our unique path. It comes to us through our feelings rather than our intellect. Our inner spirit is always leading us if we're willing to listen.

I'm always amazed at how just the right information comes to us when we need it. Many times in my work as a minister when I'd be counseling someone, I'd listen to the stories, the pain, and the challenges the person shared, and I'd wonder what I could possibly say to ease the pain, to help them take the steps they needed to take, to assist them in moving through the challenge. And then suddenly a question, an idea, or a suggestion would occur to me, as if by magic. Without having any idea what the prompting meant, I'd find that when I spoke it aloud, the person I was counseling would look at me in astonishment, burst into tears, or tell me that what I said was just what they needed to hear.

Willingness

When I am attending a ballroom dance and someone asks me to dance, I always have a choice. I can choose to sit this one out or choose to dance. If I say yes, then I'm consenting to let my partner lead, and I'm willing to follow his lead to the best of my ability.

This isn't always easy. I remember when I trusted a partner to lead and as we began to dance, I quickly realized that the dance he was leading was not the one the music called for. My resistance to dancing the wrong dance (I still like to follow the rules in certain instances in my life, and this was one of them) created an experience that was *not* one of my most enjoyable ones!

When our inner spirit asks us to dance (by guiding us to take a particular step) and we say yes, we're indicating our willingness to follow that guidance even though we may not know where that step will take us. We can always trust that our inner spirit, our divine partner, will lead us in the perfect dance for us at that moment. At a time when I was resisting the guidance I received, my inner spirit reassured me with these words:

> *Keep listening and following my guidance. Follow, no matter what I ask you to do. My guidance will never be anything that is not for your highest good and the highest good of all concerned. I assure you that my guidance will be loving, gentle, and exactly what you need. The pathway may not be the way you expect, but it will be the pathway that's necessary to move you in the direction you are meant to go.*

As I've learned to listen to and follow my inner spirit's lead, I've been delighted to hear of others who are doing the same. For instance, Jean, a student in one of my Trusting Your Inner Spirit classes shared this story:

> I was thinking about a concern in my life when my inner spirit directed me to think about my brother in Florida and his recent health challenges. I had been putting off visiting him for some time

and rationalizing about why I couldn't go. I felt a strong urge to make plans for a visit, and within a week, I was in Florida.

It was wonderful to see my brother. Because of his cognitive difficulties, we talked mostly about childhood memories. His sweet smile and his joy in sharing these memories warmed my heart. On returning home, I felt so relieved that I had made the trip, and I knew it was the right thing to do. Within four weeks, he passed from this life. I was so grateful that my inner spirit had guided me to visit him immediately.

Had Jean not been willing to listen to her inner spirit's guidance, she would have missed the chance to see her brother and share a heartwarming last visit with him.

Attentiveness

When we consent to dance, whether with a human partner in a ballroom dance or with our divine partner, the next step is to tune in. In ballroom dancing, even before the dance begins, I tune in to my partner. I assume the appropriate dance position. I wait to feel the lead my partner is providing and to feel the rhythm of the dance. I look up, not down at my feet. (Looking up helps me maintain my posture and balance during the dance.) Throughout the dance, I am attentive to the music, the beat. I pay attention to the cues my partner is giving so that I can follow with ease.

Leading and Following

I take a similar approach when I'm seeking guidance in my dance with the Divine. I tune in to my inner spirit. I look up by acknowledging that I am one with the divine presence, that I am willing to see from a higher perspective. I become still, close my eyes, and take a few deep breaths. I may focus on a question such as "What do I need to know right now?" or "What is the best choice for me at this time?" As best as I can, I let go of outer distractions and listen for the voice of my inner spirit. I pay attention to what I notice: a word or phrase that comes to my mind, an image that has meaning for me, a feeling of peace and calm, or a sense of what step I'm being guided to take.

Just as paying attention for cues in dancing takes time to master, it takes time and practice to learn to hear the still, small voice inside us. An exercise that I've found helpful in learning to listen to our inner spirit—and that I've taught to hundreds of people in my Trusting Your Inner Spirit classes—is called "What You Notice Has Meaning." It's based on the idea that everything we notice has meaning for us.

To do the exercise, close your eyes and focus on your breath for a few minutes, until you feel a sense of relaxation. Then open your eyes and observe what you notice around you. For instance, you may hear the sound of the clock ticking or birds singing, you may see the sunlight shining on a vase filled with daffodils, you may smell a vanilla candle burning, or you may experience a feeling of peace or relaxation in your body. After a few minutes, focus on three questions:

1. What did I notice?

2. What stood out for me?
3. What does what I noticed mean for me?

After doing this exercise in class, one student noticed the sound of birds singing. This stood out for her because she had not taken time to notice the birds singing in a long time. She realized that she'd been feeling very stressed for months and that connecting with nature was relaxing for her. She felt that the message from her inner spirit was to spend time outside each day, walking and paying attention to the sights and sounds around her—a simple but profound aha moment for her!

SURRENDER

In ballroom dancing, both leading and following require surrender. As a female dancer, if I want to be in the flow, I have to follow, or surrender to, my partner's lead. For both people in a physical dance, we surrender to the music, to moving together as one, to being attentive to our partner and to other dancers on the floor.

Whether we are male or female, surrendering or letting Spirit lead isn't easy. We want to be in control or at least have the illusion that we're in control. Leading implies being in control; following implies surrendering, letting go, trusting someone or something else to be in charge. In our culture, we learn that if we want to be successful, we must take control of our lives. We alone must find the solution to any and all problems, no matter how complex they may be. We must make sure the world is functioning exactly as we

Leading and Following

think it should. We learn that surrendering or letting go means losing, quitting, abdicating responsibility for our lives. But what if there is another way? What if surrendering, or letting our inner spirit lead, means releasing the need to be right and letting go of our preconceived ideas, beliefs, and judgments, our struggle, fear, and resistance? What if surrendering means allowing the power within to show us creative solutions to the challenges in our lives, guiding us to the choices that are right for us at the right time in the right way?

Have you ever had the experience of trying and trying to figure out a solution to some challenge in your life and finally surrendering (which may have felt like giving up) and deciding to take a break? Maybe you went for a walk, watched the clouds drifting by, listened to some peaceful music, or spent a few minutes meditating. Then suddenly the solution to your challenge came out of the blue. You just knew it was the perfect solution and you felt confident and relieved. If anything like this has ever happened to you, then you know what it feels like to surrender—to let go and let your inner spirit guide you. You allowed yourself to connect in a dance with the Divine.

One time when I was struggling to figure out a challenge in my life, my inner spirit told me:

As long as you think you're in control, the dance doesn't flow. When you allow me to lead you, we dance together in perfect harmony and balance.

Surrender is trusting our inner spirit and doing our part. Our human self wants to be in control; our divine self wants to surrender. Sometimes this leads to a conflict in our lives. We resist the leading of our inner spirit and attempt to control the journey that we're on.

Resistance

Because our inner spirit's guidance sometimes seems illogical and often leads us out of our comfort zone and requires change in the way we live, resistance is a natural reaction. Resistance can come in the form of thoughts such as:

- "I don't want to change."
- "What will people think?"
- "Ignorance is bliss." (If I pretend I don't hear it, I won't have to do it.)
- "Yes, but…this doesn't make sense; it isn't logical."
- "I can't really do that."
- "How do I know I didn't make it up?"
- "This is silly!"

I've found that when my inner spirit is leading me to an experience that may be uncomfortable, my initial reaction is resistance. On my first silent retreat in 1999, I became aware of this reaction. In my journal, I wrote:

> Here I am. I arrived here at the retreat center about an hour ago. It is very beautiful, and the weather is perfect. Yet I am experiencing some

anxiety about being here. Is this the right place? Why didn't I go to the shore? Maybe I should have chosen a directed retreat? Do I really want to spend seven days and six nights here? I have to share a bathroom and showers, just like a dormitory; and the bathroom is way down at the other end of the dark hall. Why didn't I start with a weekend first? Why a week?

I have to admit that my pattern of resistance to new experiences hasn't changed substantially over the years, but what *has* changed is my awareness and acceptance of it. Now I recognize resistance as part of my process. I say, "Oh, here it is again. I know I'll feel better tomorrow." And I trust that if I'm having a particular experience, it's because I was guided to it and there's something I need to learn. When I relax and don't resist the resistance, I find I'm able to move out of the place of anxiety and discomfort more quickly.

If you find yourself being resistant to following your guidance or to a new experience, you may find the following three-step process helpful in moving through resistance:

- *Breathe into the resistance.* When we feel resistance, we tend to hold our breath or breathe shallowly. Take a few minutes to breathe deeply, focusing on each inhalation and exhalation. This allows you to breathe into the resistance rather than push it away.
- *Acknowledge what you're feeling.* Are you feeling fear, doubt, guilt, anger? Acknowledging and accepting what

you feel allows you to move into the third step of moving through resistance.
- *Ask for guidance on your next steps.* Focus on two questions: "What do I need to know right now?" and "What do I need to do?"

One day when I was trying to push past the wall of resistance I was feeling toward writing my book (I had just set an intention to write for at least two hours a day, five days a week), I began to breathe into the resistance. I acknowledged that I didn't feel like writing. And I had this conversation with my inner spirit:

JULIE: What do I need to know right now?

INNER SPIRIT: *You don't feel the energy to write.*

JULIE: What do I need to do?

INNER SPIRIT: *Trust that feeling. It doesn't mean you won't want to write an hour from now, or tomorrow. It simply means that right now, in this moment, the energy isn't there for writing. Acknowledge and honor your feelings. The more you do that, the more you will feel like writing. And the writing will come from a place of desire, joy, and confidence rather than from a should or have to.*

So I followed my feelings: I went for a walk and planted a few geraniums in my garden. And to my amazement (sometimes I am still amazed by how well the process of following my inner spirit works), two hours later I was ready to write. The resistance was gone, and I spent three hours that day writing from a place of confidence and ease. I not only trusted my inner spirit, but I trusted and honored my feelings. In the process, my intention to write for at least two hours was honored as well.

STRUGGLES AND CHALLENGES

Have you ever noticed that many of the struggles and challenges in your life come from *not* letting Spirit lead? Instead of following, you may have tried to lead, to force rather than allow, in the everyday decisions of your life as well as the major changes. On several occasions while serving as minister of Unity of Palmyra, I would decide it was time to write my Sunday message. I would spend a great deal of time writing, tearing up what I wrote, and eventually giving up, only to find that several days later, after having an experience that related to my topic for the week, the words would flow and the process of writing would be easy. Perfect divine timing! (Another sign that our inner spirit is leading us in our dance with the Divine.)

Sometimes, though, my challenges as a Unity minister were far more significant than merely having a hard time writing a Sunday message. During one period, my ministry was experiencing so much conflict that I actually considered retiring. I would plan a date…it would come and go…I would plan another date…time went on, and I was still there.

I realize now that I needed to deal with the conflict that was going on in myself and in my ministry and to complete my work there before it was time to leave. Consequently, several years later, when I felt clearly guided that it was time for me to retire, I was able to leave from a place of strength for me and for our ministry, and everything in the transition process came together perfectly. Again, perfect timing when I let my inner spirit lead!

By the time I began writing this book, I thought I had learned the lesson of leading and following quite well. In ballroom dancing, I could generally follow my partners very easily and was often complimented on how well I was able to follow the leads. One partner, a beginning dancer impressed with my ability to move in the intended direction even though he wasn't sure how to lead the particular pattern, told our dance instructor that he loved dancing with me because "she just goes where she's supposed to go."

In my dance with the Divine, by this time, I had taken giant leaps in following my inner spirit's lead: leaving teaching without knowing what I was going to do next, applying for the field-licensing program leading to ordination when I didn't know if our small congregation could support me financially or emotionally in the program, and entering the Your Soulful Book program to write the book I'd been dreaming about for at least ten years. I'd been teaching the principles of trusting our inner spirit for years and firmly believed that our inner spirit can and will guide us in every aspect of our lives if we're willing to listen, trust, and follow.

Leading and Following

So, although I recognized the pattern of struggle with my ideas of how life should be vs. the guidance of my inner spirit, I was a bit surprised when I found myself struggling with following my inner spirit's lead in writing my book. All went well in the beginning until my inner spirit's wisdom didn't follow the rules of good writing that I read about or that I thought made perfect sense: creating an outline for the book, creating a hook to engage readers, having a clear idea of the format and genre of the book. Instead of focusing on word counts for the day or hours spent writing (which I tried to do nonetheless), my inner spirit would sometimes encourage me to go back and read my journals, engage in a dialogue with my inner spirit, read a particular chapter in a book, or just "sit with it" (a message my inner spirit often gave me when I needed to stop trying to figure it out and just sit in the silence, go for a walk, or do something entirely different to clear my mind). Many times, the irony of writing a book on following my inner spirit but resisting its guidance was not lost on me. However, each time I actually listened to my inner spirit's guidance, I found it very beneficial in moving past the block I was experiencing. I felt a sense of peace that I was no longer stuck, at least in that moment.

On one particular occasion when my writing was not flowing for me, I asked my inner spirit for guidance, and although it wasn't what I expected, I followed it. When I came back to my writing after a weekend break, I asked my inner spirit what it wanted me to know about my writing at the present time. I received this response in the form of a letter:

Dear Julie,

I want to thank you for following my guidance this past weekend. You were feeling discouraged, disheartened, and wanting to quit writing your book, wondering if it was really yours to do.

You sat with it and listened. You heard me say, "Put it aside for a day or two and do something completely different." So you did. You shopped, went to the farmer's market, read a novel. But most important of all, you danced! You danced at the Ballroom Break studio party on Friday night, you danced at the York USA dance yesterday, and you danced with joy. You felt good about yourself, you had fun, you felt confident and at ease. Dancing took you out of your head and trying to figure it all out and put you into your body. It was exactly what you needed!

What do you need to do today? You need to regain your confidence in your writing. You are a good writer, you are a wonderful teacher, and you need to share your insights and your wisdom in your writing. I would not have asked you to embark on this soulful book journey if I didn't feel you were the right person for this assignment. This is the right time, and you are the right person to write this book. And yes, others will want to read it and will find it inspiring, comforting, exciting,

Leading and Following

or whatever they need at the moment they read it. They will want to hear your unique voice.

No one can guide this journey but me, your inner spirit. You know that's true. Others can advise you, share their insights with you, but only your inner spirit knows what you need to say, what you need to share with the world. So, put aside others' comments, ideas, and judgments, and focus on what your inner spirit has to say.

I am with you through the struggles, the doubts, the resistance. I can move quickly or slowly or pause for a while. It's you who determines the pace by your willingness and readiness to listen. My guidance comes when you are ready to hear it. Move at the pace of guidance…the pace will be exactly what you need.

Thank you for taking time to ask me and to listen today.

Love to you,

Your Inner Spirit

Coming back to my writing that day after the weekend break, I felt refreshed, renewed, and ready to begin writing again. And guess what—my writing felt easy and effortless that day.

INNER SPIRIT NEVER GIVES UP

Even though we may resist the guidance of our inner spirit, I find it comforting to know that our inner spirit never gives up on us. It keeps giving us cues and nudges until we listen and follow.

Sometimes it seems that, almost against my will, my inner spirit picks me up and puts me where it wants me to be. This understanding was mirrored to me in a dance with my human partner some years ago. We were performing a dance routine in front of 200 people at the Valencia Ballroom in York, Pennsylvania, at the Annual Tri-Chapter Ballroom Dance Week gala. Just before the highlight of the routine—a movement in which my partner lifts me over his head and spins me around—I failed to have my leg in the proper position for him to easily lift me, a move I had done perfectly at the rehearsal and countless times before that. In the second that I hesitated, my partner picked me up—I still don't know how—lifted me into the air, and we completed the routine. Thankfully, no one but the two of us and our dance instructors realized what had happened. This experience gave me the confidence to believe that if there could be such a sense of harmony with a human dance partner, I could expect even more from my divine partner.

One of the most profound insights that's come to me through the process of listening to my inner spirit is *"The more you follow, the more I can lead you."* For me, this applies to dancing as well as to following my inner spirit. When I'm willing to follow in trust and confidence, I'm able to dance with greater joy and ease on the dance floor and in my life experiences.

DANCE STEPS TO PRACTICE LEADING AND FOLLOWING

1. Prepare to tune in to your inner spirit.

Learning to tune in to our inner spirit requires a willingness to create the time and space to be still and listen. In time and with practice, you'll be able to tune in to your inner spirit wherever you are, even in a crowd. Initially, though, when you're learning to connect with your inner spirit, you may want to set aside twenty to thirty minutes or more in a place where you can be comfortable and undisturbed. The place could be a meditation area, a favorite chair in your living room, or a calming, peaceful spot outdoors. Use whatever techniques you find helpful in relaxing your mind and body: closing your eyes, listening to soothing music, doing some stretching exercises or yoga postures, or focusing on your breath as you allow it to deepen and your body to relax.

You may want to focus on an affirmation such as:

- "I am one with the divine presence."
- "I am open and receptive to the voice of my inner spirit."
- "I am relaxed and at ease."

Give yourself the time you need to feel your body and mind relaxing.

2. Create an intention or a question to focus on.

An intention brings your heart and mind into alignment. It may be as simple as:

- "My intention is to connect with my inner spirit today."
- "My intention is to experience joy in my life."
- "My intention is to attract greater prosperity into my life."

A question may naturally follow that intention:

- "How can I connect with my inner spirit today?"
- "How can I experience more joy in my life?"
- "How can I attract greater prosperity into my life?"

When a specific intention or question is not clear to you, you may simply ask, "What do I need to know today?" and "What do I need to do?" (I find that these two questions allow me to move past what my mind thinks I want to know or do and to connect with what my inner spirit wants me to know or do.)

I find it helpful to write down the question or intention in my journal or on a piece of paper as I begin to listen for the voice of my inner spirit.

3. Listen for the voice of your inner spirit.

This step might be described best as "Stop talking and start listening." As much as possible, release the outcome of what you feel *should* happen and become open, receptive, and attentive to what *is* happening. If you're beginning the process of listening to your inner spirit, your response might be, "Nothing is happening." Don't be discouraged if you don't immediately perceive a response. It takes time and practice to learn to hear the still, small voice of your inner spirit. The more you practice, the more tuned in you will become to the voice of your inner spirit. Be aware of any images, words or phrases, feelings, or bodily sensations. Write down what you experience. Throughout the day, be attentive to answers that may come through a conversation with someone, a book you're drawn to read, or an unexpected thought or idea that seems to come out of the blue.

You might also find it helpful during this time to practice the "What You Notice Has Meaning" exercise in the "Attentiveness" section of this chapter.

4. Follow the lead—the guidance—you receive.

All the leading and all the guidance in the world is meaningless if we don't follow it. Sometimes our inner spirit will give us words of comfort, loving-kindness, or support, and the only action is to take those words into our hearts and souls. Often, though, our inner spirit will encourage us to take a step that may lead us in the direction of a dream or goal, to reach out to a friend who has been in our thoughts and prayers, or to relax and enjoy a walk in the park. Whatever the action, take the step you're guided to take. You'll find that as you take one step, you'll be guided to the next, and the next—one step at a time. When you take the step, notice how you feel, observe the results of the action. Don't be surprised if you find yourself thinking, "That is exactly what I needed."

This will happen more and more as you tune in, listen to, and follow the guidance of your inner spirit.

Chapter 6

Releasing the Imprisoned Splendor

To Dance
It took years for her to dance,
But she finally began…
Spirit leading, body following,
Body flowing, spirit soaring,
Losing herself,
Becoming her all—
She truly danced for the first time
In her life…
And she knew joy!

This verse, which I found on a plaque while wandering through a gift shop in Virginia Beach, has a special place on the wall as you enter my home. It reminds me of the freedom and joy

I felt as a five-year old child dancing around the living room in my green plaid dress and Mary Jane shoes.

Dancing has always been a part of my life, but it would be years—years that took me through the awkwardness of adolescence and junior high dances, discomfort with my non-athletic body, and fear that I might make a mistake—before I would again feel that sense of freedom and joy through dance. And it would be years before I'd understand that the same freedom comes from dancing with the Divine and letting my inner spirit lead me in my life experiences.

Feeling joy is one of the clearest signs that we are dancing with the Divine in our lives. Have you ever felt that joy in movement, in letting your body express itself freely without judgment? You may have felt it in the gentle movement of yoga or tai chi or while running through a field of newly mown grass, walking along the beach as the sun was rising, or skiing down a snow-covered hill.

Sometimes, even when we don't feel the joy of movement within ourselves, we recognize it in others. My friend Alison describes her delight in watching a five-year old girl and her father in a quaint downtown shopping area in Cape May, New Jersey.

> It was raining, and there were puddles everywhere. The little girl—dressed in pink rubber boots and a pink flowery rain jacket, her hair soaking wet—was gleefully splashing through the puddles. Her father was encouraging her to keep on keeping on. This little one was dancing in the rain, and I was fortunate enough to witness it.

Releasing the Imprisoned Splendor

Who can possibly hear this story and not think of the iconic scene from the movie *Singin' in the Rain* in which Gene Kelly dances and sings while spinning an umbrella, splashing through puddles, and getting soaked with rain? Pure joy!

I suspect that most of us would like to have more moments of dancing with the Divine, whether through physical movement or through feeling more in the flow in our daily lives. Our inner spirit can lead us to recapture the feelings of joy we may have lost through the rules, expectations, or shoulds of our lives.

My inner spirit led me to rediscover, through ballroom dancing, the joy that I'd experienced as a child dancing my way around the living room. Early on, when I was beginning to learn ballroom dancing and discovering that many of the lessons mirrored lessons I'd learned on my spiritual journey, I began receiving messages from my inner spirit about dancing:

> *I want you to dance. Dance out the fears, the pain, the hurt, the disappointments, the anger, all that keeps you from experiencing the joy within you. Don't hold back. For as you dance, you will find your own rhythm; you will find the dance of your life. You will release the imprisoned splendor within yourself, the part of you that has been lost. Dance as though nothing matters but the dance.*

"Release the imprisoned splendor"? What did that mean? How was I to find it? I intuitively knew that, for me, the words (which I recognized from the poem "Paracelsus" by Robert Browning) meant that there was more to dancing than simply learning the steps and the choreography; it was also about going deep within and finding and expressing my inner spirit, my divine essence. But how could ballroom dancing help me to release my imprisoned splendor? How can each of us learn to release our hidden splendor in our daily lives?

What Is the Imprisoned Splendor?

Have you heard the story of "The Golden Buddha"? This story (recounted in the original *Chicken Soup for the Soul* book) describes a ten-and-a-half-foot-tall Buddha statue housed in Bangkok, Thailand. For centuries, this statue was thought to be made of clay. But when it was being relocated in 1955, part of the exterior was damaged, revealing a golden surface below the exterior. The monks chiseled away the exterior until, months later, a solid gold Buddha was uncovered. It is believed that hundreds of years earlier, when the monks of Thailand were under attack from an outside force, they plastered over the statue to disguise its true worth, thereby discouraging would-be thieves. The monks of Thailand were killed by the enemy, and until 1955, the secret of the Golden Buddha was preserved.

What if each one of us has within us a Golden Buddha, an imprisoned splendor that's been covered up by fear, shame, guilt—a feeling of not being good enough (or simply not *enough*)—and our lives are the opportunity to uncover and express this imprisoned splendor? I know this is true: Inside each of us is our true self, the core of us, our divine essence, our splendor, our magnificence, our gold. What keeps us from expressing that splendor is the "clay" of life—our doubts and fears, rules, expectations, shoulds. Our task is to discover our inner splendor, chisel away all that keeps us from feeling and expressing it, and release the beauty, joy, love, and unique gifts inside us that we're meant to share with the world. Our inner spirit wants to show us how to do this so we can more fully dance with the Divine in our lives.

How Do We Release the Imprisoned Splendor Within Us?

Unfortunately, releasing our inner splendor isn't something we generally discuss at the dinner table or chat about with our family and friends. ("By the way, how did you release your inner splendor today?") However, we can ask ourselves some questions that may help us experience the feeling of releasing our imprisoned splendor: "When have I felt most in touch with my inner spirit?" "When have I felt most fully alive?" "When have I felt a sense of freedom and joy in my life?" Our feelings are guideposts to times when we have released our imprisoned splendor.

In the beginning of this chapter, you may have identified times when you felt the joy of movement. Just as we release endorphins when we move our bodies, we also are often able to let go of our inhibitions, doubts, and fears—to be fully present in the moment and get in touch with aspects of ourselves that we didn't know existed, such as our imprisoned splendor.

For me, ballroom dancing has been a process of exploring a wide variety of dances and rhythms, each one allowing me to express different aspects of myself: the fun and energetic swing dance, the perky and lighthearted mambo, the dramatic and passionate Argentine tango, and the sensual rumba. But of all the dances I've learned, the elegant, graceful, smooth-flowing waltz has been the one that's most helped me to physically embody the feeling of releasing my imprisoned splendor and dancing with the Divine.

Besides physical movement, there are many ways we may have experienced releasing our hidden splendor. Maybe it was when we were doing something we loved, like painting a breathtaking landscape, singing a favorite song that touches our soul, creating a scrumptious meal, or simply being in nature and feeling a sense of oneness with all that is.

My friend Lorrie shares her process of releasing her hidden splendor through expressing her creativity:

> I have always loved to create. As a small child, crayons were my medium. When I got older, my kitchen became my playground. I also enjoy dabbling in crafts and arranging flowers. Writing my book is my latest passion. What I appreciate about the creative process is how alive it makes me feel. It takes me out of my head, into my heart. I become one with whatever I'm creating, and I feel a oneness with the Divine. My play becomes a

meditation and the truest expression of the real me. My divine essence appears in my creation, no longer hidden from myself and the world.

Sometimes the call to release our imprisoned splendor dances us into unexpected adventures. We don't know exactly where the dance is taking us. This happened to my creative friend Kathy. Here is her story:

> As a child, I loved to paint and draw, but as an adult, I did little with that gift. One day, out of the blue, I felt a deep calling to go out into nature and examine field stones. It was so unusual, but I followed the urge. The newly plowed fields held an abundance of stones. Within the stones, I saw shapes and forms of wild creatures and had an undeniable urge to paint them. My logical mind thought, "This is absurd," but I did it anyway. Over the years, I painted a menagerie of wild animals and intuited a message from each one. It was as if each stone was unearthed to bring a message to the world, but how could that be?
>
> Then, by chance, I was invited to present a talk at a women's weekend retreat. With the stones front and center, I presented "The Wisdom of the Wild Things." I spoke of how wild nature and the qualities of wild creatures are not only outside but within us. Never before had I done a presentation where the audience was open to every word I spoke. They found the stones "magical." They laughed, they cried, they cheered, they shared their love for wild nature.

> I believe that by staying faithful to my natural creativity, I set my imprisoned splendor free. I felt the unbridled freedom of daring to express myself intuitively and instinctively. In so doing, my inner splendor touched the hearts of others. In the words of Joseph Campbell, I experienced "the rapture of being alive!"

Sometimes the feeling of releasing our imprisoned splendor comes through fulfilling a life purpose. For me, the moment of my ordination as a Unity minister was a long-awaited dream fulfilled. I've also felt this same sense of aliveness and purpose when sharing a Sunday message on God's Perfect Time, teaching a class on Trusting Your Inner Spirit, or counseling someone who's struggling with a challenge and is suddenly able to see the situation from a different perspective. Sometimes the feeling of releasing the hidden splendor has come when I'm walking in a pine-scented forest or sitting on a balcony overlooking the ocean—the sky a stunning pink, a gentle breeze blowing my hair—filling me with an experience of oneness with all that is.

Often, to release our imprisoned splendor, our inner spirit leads us to step out of our comfort zones. This happened to Dr. Maria Rothenburger, a fertility specialist:

> Years ago, I worked with a client who had lost her twins in the third trimester of pregnancy. On my way home after our first session, I had the strong impression that her babies were communicating with me. I had just begun a new meditation practice, which, I believe, helped me

connect with other realms. Eight years later, I've realized how healing it is for parents to connect with their babies both before and after birth. In July 2020, I "came out" as a spirit baby communicator, and I feel like I am now 100% myself. I had felt fearful of others' reactions; releasing that fear has led to incredible connections with my clients and many healing moments. Splendor released!

BLOCKS TO RELEASING OUR IMPRISONED SPLENDOR

Each one of us has special and unique gifts that we bring to this world to share, ways we express our authentic selves. Yet when we think about the words *release our imprisoned splendor*, we often doubt ourselves. We ask, "Who am I to think I have imprisoned splendor within myself?"

How do I know we ask ourselves this question? Because as I was writing this chapter, I too was asking myself that question. I was asking myself whether I really had to include this chapter, as it was difficult to write. I was hesitating to share that I really knew what it meant to release the imprisoned splendor and that, in fact, there were times when I *had* experienced the process in my life. Since I'm writing about trusting my inner spirit, I asked my inner spirit if it was important to include this concept. The answer was, "*Absolutely!*"

In her book *Return to Love*, Marianne Williamson beautifully expresses this hesitation to recognize and acknowledge our imprisoned splendor:

> Our deepest fear is not that we are inadequate. Our deepest fear is that we are powerful beyond measure. It is our light, not our darkness that most frightens us. We ask ourselves, "Who am I to be brilliant, gorgeous, talented, fabulous?" Actually, who are you not to be? You are a child of God. Your playing small does not serve the world. There is nothing enlightened about shrinking so that other people won't feel insecure around you. We are all meant to shine, as children do. We were born to make manifest the glory of God that is within us. It's not just in some of us; it's in everyone. And as we let our own light shine, we unconsciously give other people permission to do the same. As we are liberated from our own fear, our presence automatically liberates others.

In Louise Hay's book *You Can Heal Your Life*, she tells us that no matter what our problem, no matter why we criticize ourselves, the bottom line is the fear that we are not good enough. At first, when we compare these two views, one expressed by Marianne Williamson and one by Louise Hay, they seem to be contradictory. But maybe they are not so different after all when we remember that we are both human and divine. On a divine or spiritual level, we can feel our magnificence, our light, our splendor. We can feel that we have a divine purpose to express. But on a human level, we may feel that we don't measure up, that we aren't good enough or we aren't worthy of expressing that purpose, of being the light we're meant to be. To release our imprisoned splendor, we need to recognize the light—the divine essence—within ourselves, let go of the human fears and doubts that keep us from expressing that light, and be willing to express, or release, that divine essence into the world.

It took twenty years from the time Reverend Audrey McGinnis envisioned my becoming a Unity minister to my entering the ministerial program leading to ordination. During that time, I had to recognize the vision, the dream, within myself. I believe that my inner spirit sent me consistent messages—through my journaling, other people in my life, and glimpses of myself as a minister—until I was able to embrace the vision. Then I began to uncover and chisel away the human doubts and fears that kept me from taking the steps I needed to take (such as the feeling that I wasn't good enough or that I had to be perfect to be a minister). Finally, I had to be willing to take the steps I was guided to take to bring my dream into manifestation.

Letting Go of Perfectionism

Feeling that we aren't good enough or that we might not do it right (whatever *it* is) often leads to not doing it at all, or doing it but not experiencing the joy of it. It often leads to perfectionism, which can definitely be a deterrent to releasing our imprisoned splendor.

Many dancers are perfectionists. We want a flawless performance, to look good on the dance floor. This desire for perfection and our anxiety about making a mistake can cause tense muscles and difficulty in following a lead or moving in harmony with a partner. On the positive side, perfectionism can lead to being well organized and dependable, maintaining high standards, and aspiring to excellence. But it can also lead to self-doubt, the feeling of never being good enough (or simply being *enough*), and the fear of expressing our true selves. I often recognize that I am in perfectionist mode when I find myself saying, "I should do this" or "I shouldn't have said that."

My experiences in ballroom dancing have taught me a lot about letting go of perfectionism—during times when I've been able to let it go and during times when I haven't. One time during a dance lesson, I became discouraged and annoyed with myself because I wasn't learning a new step fast enough, or so I told myself: "I should be able to do this; I've been taking lessons for years. I shouldn't be forgetting this pattern; we've worked on it many times in the past."

As you can well imagine, this impatience with myself and my frustration with not being able to do it right didn't lead to me releasing my imprisoned splendor. Happily, however, my dance instructor, Fred—who has never been anything but patient when I've had difficulty with a step—saved the day with his soothing words: "You'll get it. It's getting better each time. Everyone has trouble with this step." Once I stopped berating myself and began believing I could do the step, I felt much more relaxed and was able to learn the step.

Sometimes when I performed my dance routines, my desire to have each one be perfect caused much worry and distress for me, often keeping me from enjoying the actual performance. On my ordination day, when I danced the waltz with my partner, Gary, I felt so excited to be performing for my congregation, family, and friends that I was totally present in the moment, dancing for the pure joy of dancing, just as I'd experienced as a five-year-old. Even though the routine wasn't technically perfect—my partner forgot to lead my favorite step, and in the beginning of the routine, I created my own step instead of the one we'd practiced—it didn't matter. I truly felt that I'd been in the divine flow, that my partner and I were not only dancing with one another, but together dancing with the Divine. The excitement I felt and the expressions of delight on the faces of those watching us more than made up for any imperfections in the dance routine.

Being totally present in the moment, experiencing joy, and not being upset by mistakes are clear signs that we're releasing our imprisoned splendor in our dance with the Divine.

In dancing, I learned that expression in dance is as important as technical performance (or doing it "perfectly"). While watching *Dancing with the Stars*, one of my all-time favorite television programs, a celebrity and her partner performed a flawless dance, very close to being technically perfect, yet something was missing. When the judges gave their critique, they applauded the flawless technique but told the celebrity, "We need to see *you*!" (In my words, we need to see you release your imprisoned splendor.)

Compare this performance with one I saw many years ago by Sarah Hughes, a sixteen-year-old figure skater, in the 2002 Winter Olympics in Salt Lake City, Utah. She dazzled the audience and the judges not only with her technical performance but with a sense of magic, of awe and wonder. Sarah was an unexpected champion who rose to release her imprisoned splendor through expressing her true self during her performance.

REMEMBERING AND FORGETTING

You may have heard the saying "Life is a process of remembering and forgetting who we are." Sometimes when we're feeling the joy of being alive—sharing our talents and gifts with one another, creating a poem or arranging flowers for a centerpiece, or simply sitting in the silence—we may feel in touch with our magnificence, our splendor. At other times, we may feel discouraged, disheartened, and doubtful that we have splendor within us. This is all part of the dance of life. The more we connect with our inner spirit, the more we remember who we are. Our inner spirit is so good at reminding us of our hidden splendor.

On a day when I was forgetting who I was, I sat in my white wicker chair in my meditation room, looking outdoors at the sunshine through the pine trees, and asked my inner spirit, "Who am I?" My inner spirit replied: "*You are light. You are love. You are my expression here on earth. You are so much more than you think you are. You can do so much more than you think you can do."*

Those few words, so lovingly spoken in the silence, are as true for you as they are for me. We are all here to express light and love and to release our imprisoned splendor into the world. This is what dancing with the Divine is all about.

Sometimes our inner spirit guides us to be reminders for one another when we forget who we are. I was the recipient of such a reminder at a time when I had forgotten who I was.

I had been facilitating a Trusting Your Inner Spirit support group of six to eight people for several years. Our focus was to learn to recognize the voice of our inner spirit, listen to it, and follow its guidance. It was also a time to affirm and recognize the inner spirit in ourselves and each other. As the facilitator, I expected myself to be a role model of how this was done. (Do I note a touch of needing to be perfect here?) One day, after a particularly challenging week, I was sharing an experience I had and criticizing myself for not handling it in the highest and best possible way. ("I should have done this. I shouldn't have said that.") One of the participants in the group looked at me with enough love to melt my heart and said, "Don't you *know* who you are?"

To this day, that acknowledgment of my spiritual essence—the imprisoned splendor within me—brings tears to my eyes and a sense of gratitude for that dear friend who reminded me of who I was when I didn't remember.

My hope is that we all can be reminders to one another of that imprisoned splendor that is in each one of us. The more we release our imprisoned splendor, the more we feel we are dancing with the Divine.

Dance Steps to Practice Releasing the Imprisoned Splendor

1. Chisel away the clay.

Like the monks who chiseled away the clay from the Golden Buddha, we need to let go of what keeps us from releasing our imprisoned splendor in our lives. Rather than making a list of everything you can think of that holds you back (which can feel overwhelming), ask your inner spirit for guidance in the moment. The question can be general (e.g., "What do I need to release in my life right now?") or very specific (e.g., "What do I need to release in order to attract a supportive, loving relationship?").

Whenever you feel fear or doubt keeping you from taking steps toward a goal or dream, take time to ask, "What's holding me back?" and "What do I need to release?"

2. Connect with the essence of who you are.

Commit to taking time in your day, even if it's just a few minutes, to listen to and connect with your inner spirit. The more you do this, the more you'll be able to get in touch with your imprisoned splendor.

St. Francis of Assisi had a special way of doing this: He would stand in front of a mirror, speak to God, and ask "Who are you, God?" He would then place his hand on his heart and ask, "Who am I?" I invite you to give this a try. If looking in a mirror feels too vulnerable (and it often does at first), you might like to ask the questions as you are walking outside observing the bright blue sky, standing in a flower garden, or drinking in the beauty of nature. Or you might simply ask, "Who am I?" as you sit in the quiet of your own special place and listen with an open heart.

3. Discover what brings you joy and make time for it in your life.

So often we get caught up in the hustle and bustle of our lives and wonder why we feel out of balance and harmony with ourselves. Feeling joy is an indication that we're in touch with our inner spirit and releasing our inner splendor. Make a list of the things that bring you joy—walking along a beach at sunset, sharing a cup of tea with a friend, reading a good book, spending time meditating—and then make time each day, even if only five or ten minutes, to engage in an activity that brings you joy. You may have so much fun doing this activity that you'll want to expand it to a half hour, a few hours each day, or one day a week.

4. Share your talents, skills, and gifts with others.

Our special talents, skills, and gifts may or may not be those with which we earn a living but often are hidden in the things we love to do, the things that give our lives purpose and meaning. You may love to share your gifts through teaching, writing, gardening, wood carving, dancing, or, in the words of Mary Manin Morrissey, simply "being a peaceful presence" in someone's life, whether through a phone call of encouragement, a handwritten note to let someone know you're thinking about them, or an email or text sharing an insight or a story they might enjoy.

What brings a sense of purpose and meaning to your life? How have you shared your talents and gifts with others in a way that made you—and the receiver—feel empowered, supported, loved? When have you felt most fully alive, as though you were dancing with the Divine? Identify at least ten times in your life when you've felt these feelings. Are you experiencing moments like this in your life now? If not, what step can you take in the next forty-eight hours to share your talents and gifts in a way that brings you this sense of purpose and meaning? Ask your inner spirit for guidance. (Our inner spirit will often guide us to just the right gift at the right time.)

5. Live in the moment.

One of the ways I've found most helpful in releasing the hidden splendor in my life is to create unstructured time, time in which I'm free to follow the energy in the moment—nothing planned, nothing I have to do. Unstructured time allows us to focus on being fully present in each moment, to listen to our bodies, our emotions, our inner spirit. I invite you to set aside a few hours, an afternoon, or even a full day for unstructured time. For this time, put aside all distractions—the phone, the to-do list, the obligations and shoulds. Focus on sitting in a comfortable chair, taking a few deep breaths, and listening to your body and your emotions. (Remember, our inner spirit speaks to us through our physical and emotional bodies.) What does your body need right now? A walk, a glass of water or something warm to drink, time to rest and pamper yourself? Follow your body's lead and notice how you feel. Ask questions such as, "What would I like to do right now?" Do it and see how you feel. Continue to ask, "What would I like to do right now?" Keep following and noting your feelings. If you find yourself saying, "That is exactly what I needed," you are definitely following your inner spirit. If this process is new to you, don't be surprised if you have no idea what you feel or want to do. We can become so used to doing what's expected of us or what we feel we should do that it can take time to learn to follow the energy in the moment. You can practice this in your daily life by pausing throughout the day and asking:

- "What do I need right now?"
- "What decision will bring me peace right now?"
- "How can I be a loving, peaceful presence right now?"

6. Live authentically.

Nothing helps us release our imprisoned splendor more than being true to ourselves—speaking our truth, honoring our own unique path in this world, being willing to trust our inner spirit to guide us. When we feel at peace, when we feel in harmony with ourselves, when we know we've acted in accordance with our highest truth, then we know we're living authentically.

Questions are a wonderful way of connecting with our inner spirit, which is why I so often include them in this book's "dance steps." When we ask questions with an open heart and a willingness to receive an answer that may be unexpected, we learn so much about who we really are.

Think about a situation in your life in which you're not being true to yourself. Maybe you're trying to please others or are about to make a decision based on what you think you should do but that doesn't feel right to you. Ask one or more of these questions:

- "What is right for me?"
- "What is most important to me right now?"
- "How can I express myself in the highest and best possible way in this situation?"

Once again, think of the situation where you're not being true to yourself, but this time imagine yourself responding in the most authentic way possible for you. Observe how you feel as you respond from this authentic place inside you, from your splendor. Continue visualizing yourself in this situation until you feel empowered to speak and act from your authentic self.

7. Take a step out of your comfort zone.

Our inner spirit often guides us to step out of our comfort zones in order to stretch and grow so we can release our imprisoned splendor. Without the guidance of my inner spirit, I would never have danced at my ordination, left my teaching position without knowing what I was going to do next, or applied to ministerial school. I would have missed opportunities to feel the freedom and joy of releasing my imprisoned splendor.

Is there something you've been feeling guided to explore—taking ballroom dance lessons, learning to play the guitar, volunteering at a childcare center, white-water rafting, or going to the seashore by yourself for a personal retreat—but have resisted because you think you don't have the time, you probably wouldn't be good at it, or it just isn't you? Now is the time to chisel away at those doubts and fears and take a step out of your comfort zone. Ask yourself, "What would I choose to do if time, energy, and money weren't issues?" and "If I knew I couldn't fail, what would I like to do?"

What brings you a feeling of excitement and passion (and probably a bit of doubt and fear) just by thinking about it? Once you've identified what this is for you, ask, "What small step could I take to move me toward this dream?" Maybe it's to explore ballroom dance studios in your area, volunteer opportunities in your chosen field, or retreat centers that offer personal retreat weekends. What's one step that you're willing to take? Take that step now. You'll be amazed at how one step will lead to another—and another and another—until you find yourself out of your comfort zone and into new possibilities in your dance with the Divine.

Chapter 7

Flowing with Divine Timing

When I'm learning a new dance—whether it's a sensual rumba, a playful cha-cha, or a graceful foxtrot—a magical process of transformation happens inside me. I move from consciously coordinating basic steps of the dance with the beat of the music to *feeling* the beat of the music in my body, mind, and spirit. By the end of this process, I'm expressing myself through the movement of the dance. No matter how much I try, I can't force this perfect timing to occur. It comes with practice, persistence, and a willingness to be open and vulnerable. When I'm dancing with a partner, we must, at the very least, move to the same beat. When we're both in harmony with the music and with each other, something almost mystical occurs. It's as if, together, we become one with the music, and the dance flows with grace and ease.

Have you felt this sense of perfect timing—divine timing—in your own life? A time when you just happened to be at the right place at the right time? A time when everything in your life seemed to be in harmony, when you felt in the flow of life, that all was right in your world? A time when you waited and waited for a longing of your heart to be fulfilled, and when it finally happened, you knew, without a shadow of a doubt, that the dream fulfilled was worth waiting for?

My friend Leslyn felt this sense of perfect divine timing while visiting with her new granddaughter:

> I had not been able to see my beloved granddaughter Nora the first few months of her life. Finally, the day came when I was able to have her visit in my home. As I was sitting on my rocking chair, feeding and holding her, surveying the scene I had imagined for so long, I had the feeling that I was at the right place, doing the right thing, at the right time. All was well in my world. This day—this moment—was worth waiting for!

In our dance with the Divine, our inner spirit is the guiding force in divine timing. The more we listen to, trust, and follow our inner spirit, the more we find ourselves in the right place at the right time, feeling as though all is well in our world.

I discovered the magic of being at the right place at the right time in my dance with the Divine in 1999 when I experienced my first silent retreat—seven days of silence at the Jesuit Retreat Center in Wernersville, Pennsylvania. Each morning, my inner spirit would give me a theme for the day, which I would faithfully write in my journal, eagerly anticipating the insights and adventures I would write about that day. My themes—overcoming resistance, becoming aware of blocks, seeing possibilities, surrendering, discerning divine will, resting and renewal, and completion—were exactly what I needed each day. Throughout the day, I'd be guided throughout the spacious grounds to places and experiences related to the theme for the day.

Noticing the Nudge

On the third day of my retreat, the theme is "seeing possibilities." After I write the theme in my journal, I feel an inner nudge, as if I'm ever so gently being taken by an invisible hand and led to a cloistered walkway overlooking the beautiful, spacious grounds of the retreat center. From here, I can see the whole area from a different perspective. What a perfect way for my inner spirit to show me that seeing possibilities is about seeing from a higher perspective!

Although I've already walked the grounds many times, today I'm led to places I haven't seen before or to observe something I haven't noticed before. As I notice a place, I move toward it, and I discover that each place has a message for me at that moment. It's up to me, with the help of my inner spirit, to discern what that message is.

I notice a statue of Mary holding baby Jesus. As I move toward it, I discover a clear path to the statue; I don't have to trudge through the thick grass, which yesterday, I thought was my only option to arrive at my destination. I sit on the bench beside the statue—a bench that was occupied the previous two days when I wanted to sit there to reflect. It seems that at the right time in the right way, the path opened up for me. Aha! My inner spirit is showing me another possibility. If I trust that at the right time, in the right way, a path will open up for me that I can't yet see—one that will be easy and effortless, that I won't have to force or try to make happen—how much easier the waiting will be.

Throughout the day, I'm inspired with ideas for workshops, talks, and retreats I can use in my ministry at Unity of Palmyra. I call these ideas "divine ideas" because they come from the Divine, from my inner spirit.

Today the possibilities seem to dance in my head. To capture them, I write them in my journal. By the end of this day, I've discovered that there are endless opportunities for me when I allow my inner spirit to lead me and am open and receptive to seeing possibilities.

Later, I'll reflect on these options, noticing which ones call to me—which are like seeds planted in my mind and heart. I'll listen for any steps I may be guided to take to bring these desires into manifestation. I'll follow that guidance one step at a time. I'll trust that, as a seed blossoms into a full-grown flower, at exactly the right time, the desire of my heart will manifest in my life.

TIMING IS EVERYTHING

During this seven-day retreat, I filled my journal pages with insights and messages I received from my inner spirit. One of the most memorable entries for me is the definition I was given for divine timing.

> Timing is everything. Divine timing is the time when all things come together in perfect harmony for the highest good of all concerned—so perfectly that it could not be orchestrated by human effort. You must be willing to be still and listen, to follow the guidance you receive, and then act or wait according to divine guidance.

At the end of my retreat, when silence was no longer required, I talked with one of the novices in the Jesuit Retreat Center program. I shared with him the themes I'd received from my inner spirit for each day. To my amazement, he told me that the themes were very similar in name and order to those that were part of the prescribed program for silent retreat for Jesuit priests. I don't know about you, but I call that magic—the magic that comes as a result of listening to and following our inner spirit. Divine timing was definitely at work in my life during that retreat, and I began to understand and trust in this principle and its workings in my life. Although I didn't have words to describe the process yet, I was learning what it felt like to dance with the Divine, to let my inner spirit guide me in a beautiful divine flow.

As you look back at the decisions you've made in your life, can you see the perfection of divine timing? Can you identify times when you felt in the divine flow of life? Sometimes we can only see perfect timing in retrospect. As I look back at my dance with the Divine, I see the perfection of divine timing in my decision to leave the West Shore School District after eighteen years, to apply to the field-licensing program at Unity Worldwide Ministries, to find the location for our new church in Palmyra, and to retire after twenty-five years of ministry. In all these decisions, first came the idea or possibility in my consciousness, then the struggle to decide when and how to take the action required, and finally the feeling of certainty that it was the right time and the right place, as guided by my inner spirit. I've learned that the more I'm willing to listen to, trust, and follow my inner spirit, the more confident, at ease, and in the flow of life I feel.

A Time of Waiting

One of the challenges of divine timing is that it often involves a time of waiting—waiting for an answer to a prayer, waiting for a desire to be fulfilled, waiting for a goal to be reached. And most of us aren't good at waiting. We live in a world of instant gratification where information is available on the internet twenty-four hours a day, seven days a week; microwaves heat our food in a matter of minutes; instant credit allows us to buy that new car or video game. Even when faced with waiting in a line at the grocery store or the bank, we find ourselves moving from line to line in hopes of avoiding time spent waiting (or as Sue Monk Kidd describes it in *When the Heart Waits*, "avoiding the misery of standing still").

What further complicates divine timing for us is that it's not necessarily the same as our human concept of time. At this point, you may be asking, "What does *that* mean?" Let me explain.

In the Greek language, there are two words for time: *chronos*, meaning chronological time or clock time, and *kairos*, meaning the right or opportune time, or spiritual time. Our world works on chronos time—logical, sequential, orderly, human-created time. Divine timing works on kairos time—governed by divine order, the understanding that there is a harmonious, purposeful order to our world that is always moving us in the direction of our highest good. Kairos time, unlike chronos time, can't be planned or forced. It often involves waiting. In our dance with the Divine, we often hear the phrases "waiting for God," "waiting for divine guidance," or "moving at the pace of guidance." For those of us who already dislike the concept of waiting, this isn't appealing. What if the guidance never comes? What if we wait too long and the opportunity passes us by? What if…what if…what if?

Do you remember, as a child, sitting in the back seat of your family car during a road trip and calling out to your mom and dad, "How long will it take until we get there?" "How much farther do we have to go?" "Are we there yet?" As adults, we still want to know exactly how long we'll have to wait to have what we want or to move through a situation that we want to end. The familiar phrase

"It will take as long as it takes," provides very little comfort for most of us when we're waiting.

When I left my position as a reading specialist in the 1990s and was in the process of discerning what to do from day to day, I sometimes felt that I wasn't making any progress, that I was standing still. My inner spirit had this to tell me:

> *Sometimes standing still is the best possible choice until you feel the gentle push to move in another direction. It's also the most difficult. Sit with it until you feel the clarity to move forward. Sometimes standing still is gathering the momentum to move forward. Move in the direction you feel guided to move in and all will be well.*

There was that phrase again: "sit with it." This time, my inner spirit was telling me to be patient and wait until I had clear guidance to move forward. I have to admit that this process of sitting with it is remarkably effective, but it's *not* always what I want to hear when I'm feeling impatient and wanting an answer right then and there.

WHY WAIT?

Believe it or not, as difficult as waiting is for most of us, it does have benefits. Like Leslyn visiting with her granddaughter for the first time, you may have experienced the feeling of "it was worth waiting for" in your own life following the birth of a child, finding your soulmate after seemingly endless years of dating, receiving the job offer of your dreams after months of futile searching. At that moment of fulfillment, you may have forgotten the fears and doubts you felt while you were waiting for the dream to manifest. But how do we find the benefits in the waiting process itself?

Like the void stage in a transition—that time between an ending and a new beginning—waiting for divine timing to work its magic is a time to reflect, to become clear on what's important to us, what we truly desire. Remembering the definition of divine timing that my inner spirit gave me during my silent retreat—*"Divine timing is the time when all things come together in perfect harmony for the highest good of all concerned"*—has given me food for thought in times of waiting. What if the time of waiting is occurring because what we desire is not yet ready for us? What if the time of waiting is giving us time to grow, to prepare in consciousness for what we desire? What if the time of waiting is a time to step back and see a situation in our lives with greater clarity and understanding?

The process of moving into our new church home at Unity of Palmyra revealed to me the benefits of waiting. When our congregation was given the church building, there was a six-month period between our being given the building and the time we could move in. During that time, we moved from a space we'd outgrown at the Best Western Inn to a much larger space at a nearby Comfort Inn. This six-month period gave us time to grow our congregation from a group of twenty-five to a group of more than sixty people. It also gave us time to grow in the consciousness of what we needed to do before becoming a full-time ministry. (The excitement of knowing we'd have our own church building in six months created new growth and new ideas in our spiritual community.) During this time, a transformation was occurring that wasn't apparent until we moved into our new church home.

Sometimes, in the period of waiting, growth is occurring even though we may not be aware of it until later. The caterpillar in the chrysalis is a perfect example of this. When we look at the chrysalis from the outside, it appears as though nothing is happening, but *inside* the chrysalis, growth and change is occurring. The caterpillar is undergoing a metamorphosis, which ultimately leads to a new life as a butterfly!

Waiting for the Divine Push

Because we live in a fast-paced world, we're often encouraged to move quickly and make spur-of-the-moment decisions without considering the consequences. If we move ahead without feeling confirmation deep within, without knowing that the choice we make is the right one, we often feel regret. Who has not looked back at a decision made in haste and said, "Oh, if only I had waited; if only I had trusted that I would be guided at the right time in the right way"? The idea of waiting until we feel certain, taking time to consider all the options, or even saying "No, I'm not ready" is foreign to many of us.

Flowing with Divine Timing

Many times in my life, I've pushed myself to do things I wasn't ready for—learning to drive at sixteen years old because everyone else was learning, getting married to someone when it didn't really feel right to me, sending for an application for the field-licensing program because I thought it was time. I wasn't trusting my own process. I've learned that being ready is an awareness that doesn't come from just the body or the mind but from the whole of me—body, mind, and spirit in alignment.

This lesson has been confirmed for me in ballroom dance lessons. Sometimes I've tried to learn a new step or pattern but no matter how many times I practiced it, I just couldn't get my arms and feet coordinated. It was as if my mind was telling me I couldn't possibly do this movement, my body responded in kind, and my emotions ranged from determination to frustration, making me want to give up and forget the whole thing. Fortunately, at these times—and usually before I began to scream in anger—my instructor would patiently say, "Let's let it go for now and come back to it later."

A week later, a month later, or sometimes many months later, we'd come back to the movement, and I would wonder, "Why in the world did I think this was so difficult?"

Sometimes we may find it hard to know when divine timing is right. Years ago, while having doubts about whether to apply for the Unity Worldwide Ministries Field Licensing Program, I journaled about my feelings:

> I feel as though I can't move forward and I don't know whether the resistance I feel is a sign to stop, to push through, or to wait.

My guidance was:

> *Go within to the quiet of your own being. I know you're feeling afraid right now, but remember that you are not alone. Remember the perfection of divine timing and trust it! Perhaps all the information you need to make the decision isn't yet here. So, the answer is not to stop (at least not permanently). It is not to push through. The answer is to wait. Wait in the consciousness of knowing that all is in divine order. Wait until you feel the divine push to act. In the meantime, do what is yours to do. The time isn't right to make a decision now.*

This guidance confirmed what I was feeling and helped me feel more peaceful, calm, centered, and trusting. I know that when I work against divine timing in my life by pushing, worrying, doubting, or trying to force things to happen, it's like trying to walk against a strong headwind. But when I trust the process and allow divine timing to do its perfect work, the wind seems to be blowing behind me, ushering me forward in the right direction. Until the time was right, I took the steps I felt guided to take. I talked to my congregation about supporting me in the field-licensing process. We began to look beyond our rented space at the Best Western Inn for a permanent home where we could grow our membership, establish a youth education program, and enjoy fellowship activities. I continued to journal, ask for guidance, and take the steps I was guided to take. By the time I applied and was accepted into the field-licensing program two years later, my congregation was fully committed to supporting me in the process, we had found our new church home, and I had worked through many of my doubts and fears about becoming an ordained minister. Divine timing was perfect—all things came together in perfect harmony for the highest good of all concerned.

Years later, after serving as a Unity minister at Unity of Palmyra for twenty-five years, I was contemplating retirement. Letting go of the ministry I had founded and the congregation I had loved for many years wasn't easy for me. Frequently, I would ask, "Is this the time for me to leave?" I would immediately follow that question with, "I'm not ready yet. I can't leave my spiritual family." My prayer was that when it was the right time for me to leave, I would know, without a doubt.

One day in the spring of 2016, I was sitting in the sanctuary of our church, gazing at the stained-glass windows, feeling the peace and harmony I always felt there. Gently and lovingly, I heard the words from deep within myself, *It is time for you to leave*. This time my response was different because I was ready and I knew it was time. I simply said the words, "I know." I felt a sense of peace and confidence in the choice I was making.

Within a year, I retired from Unity of Palmyra. It was the right time. The transition process, although filled with times of joy and sadness, was mostly smooth and easy. A transitional minister, who went on to become the new minister, was hired, and I completed my time there in an atmosphere of appreciation and love.

Flowing with the River

Because we're so oriented to chronos time in our lives, I'm often asked about divine timing in my Trusting Your Inner Spirit classes: "How can I align with divine timing?" "How can I know it's working in my life?" I love the Chinese proverb "Don't push the river; it flows by itself." To me, this is a perfect analogy for aligning with divine timing. Like the river, divine timing flows by itself, but we have the choice of whether to flow with it or against it.

Years ago, I learned about flowing with the river when my cousin Kelly took me tubing down the Delaware River in Bucks County, Pennsylvania. Not being an athletic person and wondering why in the world she chose this activity for fun, I was skeptical about my ability to complete a two-hour journey downstream. All went smoothly until the river wasn't flowing as quickly as I thought it should.

To help it along, I began paddling furiously with my arms and legs. Each time I did this, I ended up in the rocks along the shoreline. And each time this happened, I'd look over at Kelly and see her floating along smoothly and easily.

Finally, I got the message. I stopped trying to push against the river and allowed myself to flow with it. Once I did this, I felt relaxed and peaceful, in harmony with the flow of the river. And I actually enjoyed the ride!

Being in the flow of divine timing is like this journey on the river. If we're pushing, forcing, trying to make life behave as we think it should, we feel frustrated, overwhelmed, confused, out of harmony with ourselves and with life. But if we're letting go and allowing the natural flow of life to lead us and trusting that everything is happening exactly as it's meant to, then we feel relaxed, calm, confident, and in harmony with ourselves and with life.

You may find these three steps helpful in being in the flow of divine timing:

1. Aligning with your heart's desire

What do you really want to do, be, or have in your life? The answers come not in making a quick list as we dash off to the next item on our to-do list but in taking time to be still and listen to the voice of our inner spirit. What is important to you? What makes your heart sing? What is your inner spirit guiding you to do or be? Then, guided by our inner spirit and in harmony with the desires of our heart, we set an intention, a focus for moving forward. That intention might be to find a supportive, loving relationship; to experience greater joy in life; or to express greater creativity in the work we do.

2. Letting go and allowing divine timing to do its work in your life

Just as I had to let go of pushing the river and trying to control how quickly I could get where I was going on my tubing journey, we have to let go of worrying and trying to make life happen in our own way and in our own time. We release our notions of when, where, and how our desired good should come about. Often, what we desire doesn't happen the way we expect or in the time frame we're expecting. After creating an intention or envisioning my heart's desire, I like to affirm, "This or something better." (Sometimes the Universe has a better idea for us than any we could have imagined for ourselves.)

3. Trusting that there's always enough time, energy, money, and resources—whatever is needed—to do what you're guided to do

We trust that everything happens in its perfect time. Since the only time we have is the present moment, we align with divine timing by asking in each moment, "What is mine to do right now?" "What action do I need to take right now?" When we take the step we're guided to take in each moment, the next step appears naturally without our having to control or make it happen.

When I find myself wavering in my trust in divine timing, I find comfort and reassurance in this anonymous quote: "Your life has a divine purpose. Trust that your path [or your dance with the Divine] is unfolding as it should…in God's time, not yours."

When we feel a sense of peace, confidence, and trust that everything in our lives is working exactly as it's meant to, we know we're aligned with divine timing. When we begin to see synchronicities happening in our lives—we meet just the right person to answer a question we asked, we read a passage in a book that explains exactly what we need to know, we find a want ad in the Sunday newspaper leading us to our new church home—we know we're aligned with divine timing. When we no longer feel the need to push and force and make life happen, when we're able to wait for our hearts' desires to manifest without fear, doubt, or anger, we know we're aligned with divine timing. When we feel in the divine flow of life, in harmony with our inner spirit, we know we're aligned with divine timing.

DANCE STEPS TO PRACTICE DIVINE TIMING

1. Align with the divine presence.

I have always loved the quote, "Put God in the center, and it will all come together." Take time each day to be still and listen to the voice of your inner spirit. When we're centered in the divine presence, in touch with our inner spirit, we feel the assurance that all is well. We have the patience to wait and trust. We can see from a higher perspective. When we're waiting, it's so easy to get caught up in negativity. Let your inner spirit lead you to focus on the positive. You may be led to pray, meditate, use positive affirmations, read inspirational material, walk in nature, or listen to soothing music. Notice how you feel after following the guidance of your inner spirit. When you're aligned with the divine presence, there's a feeling of calm, peace, and confidence in the process.

2. Move at the pace of guidance.

If you're feeling rushed, overwhelmed, confused, frustrated, it's time to slow down, pause, or even stop. As Christina Baldwin shares in her book *Seven Whispers,* "We can trust that in stopping, the wisdom for proceeding will find us." Stop worrying, stop trying to figure it out, stop trying to make it happen, and be still. Ask, "What do I need right now?" Maybe the answer is a phone call with a friend, maybe it's a walk in the woods, or maybe it's to put aside a project you're working on until you feel clear about the best way to complete it. As you take time to be still and listen to the voice of your inner spirit, you'll be guided as to the steps to take at the pace that is right for you.

3. Notice the progress that is occurring.

While you're in the period of waiting, look for ways in which your prayer has already been answered, your intention is already being met, and positive changes are already occurring.

- What good is already happening?
- What inner changes are you seeing in yourself?
- How are you seeing the situation in a new way?
- Are you feeling more at peace, more loving?

When we're willing to look, we can always find some small measure of good in any situation. The more we focus on that good, the more we draw the positive into our lives. What we focus on expands.

4. Ask questions.

If you're feeling stuck or frustrated or you think that nothing is happening while you're waiting, remember that your inner spirit loves questions, especially when you wholeheartedly want to receive an answer.

Questions can help us see from another perspective or change something in ourselves that may be holding us back from manifesting our desires. Questions like these may be helpful in bringing you clarity:

- "What do I need to do or change in myself to bring about what I desire or to receive the answer to my prayer?"
- "What behavior pattern or belief do I need to release?"
- "How can I see this situation differently?"

If you sincerely ask a question and want to know the answer, you will receive an answer. If you take action on the answer you receive, that action moves you forward in a positive direction, often instantaneously.

5. Live in the moment.

In divine timing, we're exactly where we need to be in each moment. There's nothing that keeps us in the divine flow more than savoring each moment, whether we're drinking a soothing cup of hot chocolate, relaxing on a lawn chair overlooking a serene lake, or feeling totally engrossed in a favorite book. In the present moment, there's no room for worry, fear, doubt, or regret. When you find your thoughts lingering in the past or drifting into the future, bring your attention back to your present surroundings. Notice what you see, hear, smell, taste, and feel. Be aware of any actions you feel guided to take in the moment. Will taking that action bring you peace, love, joy? The more you choose to act from a positive place within yourself, the more you'll feel in the flow of perfect divine timing.

Chapter 8

It's All About Trust

In a 1982 *Frank and Ernest* comic strip, cartoonist Bob Thaves created the often-quoted phrase, "Ginger Rogers did everything that Fred Astaire did. She just did it backwards and in high heels." Talk about trust! Ginger had to trust her partner to lead her away from obstacles on the dance floor and keep her from backing into other couples—all while guiding her through very complicated choreography.

As a ballroom dancer, I've learned the importance of trust. When I dance with a partner, I trust that he'll know the steps, be able to lead me in a way that I can follow, and be patient if we don't do the dance perfectly. Maybe we can even learn to laugh at our mistakes. I often feel very vulnerable in dancing with a partner—I am literally putting myself in his hands, trusting that he will respect me as a person as well as a dance partner.

Every aspect of ballroom dancing involves trust. For me, this included choosing a dance instructor who not only was trained and qualified in teaching dance but who would be patient with me, have my well-being in mind, and be willing to move at my pace—someone with whom I felt comfortable and at ease. It also included choosing dance partners who were interested in learning and growing in dance, were willing to put in the time needed to perform routines, and were considerate and fun to be with. (After all, we'd be spending lots of time together—I wanted it to be enjoyable!) And perhaps most importantly, it meant trusting myself—when learning a dance step or pattern was difficult for me, trusting that after a time and with enough practice, I'd learn what I needed to.

When we trust our partner in ballroom dancing, there's a feeling of ease, of being in the flow, of moving together as one, of greater energy and vitality. So it is when we trust our inner spirit. We feel as if we're dancing an exquisitely choreographed waltz, in perfect harmony with our divine partner. In a graceful dance with the Divine, we trust that if we ask our inner spirit for guidance and take time to listen, we'll receive that guidance at the right time and in the right way. We trust that we'll be able to follow the guidance we receive. We trust that whatever happens is meant to happen. We learn to trust the process.

CAN YOU FEEL THE TRUST?

When have you felt this trust with your inner spirit? I've felt this trust when I receive an inner nudge to call a friend who needs to talk with me, and I find that I have just the right words she

It's All About Trust

needs to hear during a challenge in her life. I've felt this trust when I hear that it's time to leave work for home because a snowstorm is on its way, and I get home just as the winding hill leading up to my home is becoming slippery and dangerous to travel. I've felt this trust when I'm guided to go to a dance even though I'd rather stay home with a good book, and after I get to the dance venue, realize that the exercise and connection with friends is just what I need.

Maybe you've had a similar experience. You may have felt this trust when you've set an intention or asked a question of your inner spirit and received a result that brought you the exact results you were hoping for. Or maybe you've felt this trust when you allowed results to be different from what you expected...but, in retrospect, exactly what you needed.

I've found that asking my inner spirit questions—and being open to whatever it tells me—creates a beautiful dance of trust. When feeling out of harmony with myself, I've asked my inner spirit, "What can I do to feel more at peace right now?" One time, I heard the response, "*Put on your* Sounds of the Sea *CD and just let the music gently soothe you.*" I listened to my inner spirit and to the music, and I felt more relaxed and at peace. When I've been writing and have felt stuck in my head, I've paused and asked my inner spirit, "What do you want me to share today?" The guidance I've received has led me from my head to my heart—and when I'd return to my writing, the words would flow from my heart.

Don't you just love it when you ask your inner spirit for guidance and the answer comes quickly? Even if you don't hear an immediate response, the answer may come later that day in a book you're reading, in a conversation with a friend, or in a song you hear on the radio. I've found that the more aware I am of my question and the more open I am to receiving an answer, the more everything I notice has meaning. I may notice that I'm singing a song from my childhood and ask myself, "What meaning does this song have for me now?" I may be aware of body signals, such as a headache, or tension in my neck or shoulders, and realize it's a signal that the path I'm taking isn't the right one for me.

Focusing on the question seems to draw synchronicities to me. I may run into someone I was just thinking about and who has an answer I'm looking for, or I'll just happen to be at the right place at the right time for a job opportunity I didn't even know existed.

Challenges Along the Way

It's easy to trust our inner spirit when the results are what we want or expect, when we receive answers immediately, or when things are going our way. But when a challenge arises—a loved one dies, a relationship ends, or we don't get the results we anticipated—we doubt ourselves. We question our ability to follow the guidance of our inner spirit. Even worse, we doubt the guidance we were given. This happened to Carol, a young woman who felt she was following her inner spirit, but the results were not what she expected them to be.

I'd been guest speaking at a Sunday service at a Unity church. My message topic was "Trusting Your Inner Spirit." After the service, Carol approached me, looking very puzzled and upset. She told me she thought she had trusted her inner spirit in entering into a relationship with her significant other, only to find that the relationship had ended after two years. My response was—and I hope I said it in a loving way—"What makes you think you didn't trust your inner spirit?" She looked doubtful as she turned and walked away. I could tell it wasn't the response she'd hoped for. Several months later, Carol appeared at another class I was teaching. This time, she had a different perspective on the question I had asked her. When she asked for guidance on the relationship, she expected that the relationship would last forever, and when it didn't, she was convinced that her guidance was wrong. When she thought about it, she realized that the two years she had with her partner were filled with much love and that she had learned and grown in the relationship. She was grateful she'd had the experience even though it didn't last forever.

Following our inner spirit doesn't mean we won't experience obstacles along the way. My friend Linda, after being diagnosed with a tumor on her right lung, felt very strongly that her inner spirit was guiding her to treat the condition holistically, using prayer, homeopathy, and vitamin supplements.

Her medical doctor, convinced that the tumor was malignant, told her that if she didn't have a biopsy followed by chemotherapy and radiation, she wouldn't live to see another year. Despite her doctor's warning, Linda proceeded with the plan that she felt was right for her. Her holistic treatments took months to begin to have any effects, yet Linda continued to trust that she was being guided.

Ultimately, her courage and willingness to follow guidance led to the tumor disappearing and to a full recovery for her.

When we encounter an obstacle on our path, instead of viewing it as a message to stop and take another course of action, we might see the obstacle as meaningful information or as a catalyst for asking important questions such as: "What do I need to pay attention to?" "What attitude do I need to change?" "How committed am I to the path I am on?" "Is there a better way?" The obstacles Linda encountered strengthened her resolve that the path she was taking was the right path for her.

Radical Trust

Trusting our inner spirit doesn't necessarily mean being free of doubts; it means being willing to act as guided in spite of our doubts. In the process of learning to trust my inner spirit, there have been many times when I've struggled with self-doubt. Sometimes self-doubt comes in the form of hitting a wall—an obstacle or challenge that seems to stop or impede our progress. Sooner or later, in the process of learning to trust our inner spirit, we all encounter walls in our lives. What we decide to do with these walls and how we choose to see them determines whether we *get* through them or *grow* through them to greater clarity, confidence, and courage in our lives. Sometimes this process requires radical trust.

I'd just finished writing the first draft of my book (which all writers know is only the beginning of a long process of rethinking, rewriting, revising, and editing countless times until the book is born into the world). Instead of focusing on how far I'd come (I had the courage to join the Your Soulful Book program; I had begun to write the book I'd been guided to write for years; I had completed my first draft), I focused on all that still needed to be done, which left me feeling overwhelmed and discouraged.

One night I had a dream that ultimately was a turning point in trusting my inner spirit in my writing and in my life:

> I'm climbing a twenty-by-thirty-foot wall. I'm about two-thirds of the way up the wall. I'm feeling discouraged, exhausted, unwilling to continue the arduous climb. I tell myself, "I can't do this. I don't want to do this. It's too hard." I give up and go back down to the foot of the wall. I decide to take a train ride, which takes me part way around the wall. Next, I find a car, and although I have no idea which direction to take, I manage to cross a bridge that takes me back to the wall. Again, I stand at the foot of the wall, where a line has now formed to climb the wall. A gentleman standing in front of me in the line hears my litany of complaints—"I can't, I don't want to, It's too hard"—and assures me that climbing the wall is the only way to get to the other side.

When I wake up, I wonder why I believed there was only one way to get to the other side of the wall when I'd just taken a train and driven a car to the other side. Although dreams aren't always logical, they usually have a meaning for us. I knew this dream had a valuable lesson for me about climbing the wall in my life.

So, what do we do when we hit a wall in our lives? Often, we try to push our way through the wall—trying to make the situation work by doing more of what we've been doing (in my case, make myself write even if it means sitting at my computer staring into space for my two hours of allotted writing time). We get angry at the wall: "Why is this delay happening? I don't have time for this nonsense right now!" Sometimes we try to deny that the wall exists: "There is no wall. Everything's fine. The wall will disappear tomorrow." After trying all these options, I paused and made time to listen to my inner spirit. This was the message I received:

> *This is a time for radical trust. You are writing a book about trusting your inner spirit. Which do you trust more, your inner spirit or the shoulds, the expectations, the rules you think you must follow? What if you totally trusted your inner spirit to lead you through this process of moving through the wall? If you are willing to dance with me in this process, I can show you how to move through any wall with grace and ease.*

Oh, yes, a timely reminder that our inner spirit is always giving us opportunities to learn to trust more. I knew it was time for radical trust. There was a message here for me to uncover, a message that was important for me and could be beneficial for others to hear as well.

Over the next few months, as I began to spend more and more time listening, journaling, and practicing what I was learning, a four-step process emerged as a guide in growing through a wall in our lives and in deepening our trust in our inner spirit. Although my guidance revealed the process to me in four distinct steps, I've found that I often move through the steps concurrently and sometimes, doing any one of the steps—usually seeing from a higher perspective—will bring me the clarity I need to move forward.

As you read the four steps, you may notice that I use the word *willing* numerous times. This isn't by chance. In our dance with the Divine, willingness is a key component as we learn to listen to, trust, and follow our inner spirit. Willingness is a commitment to being open and receptive to a process that may sometimes confuse us, challenge us, and inspire us to grow.

Step 1: Over the Wall

During my spiritual retreat at the Jesuit Retreat Center in 1999, I was guided to a balcony overlooking the spacious grounds of the center so that I could see from a higher perspective. When we climb *over* a wall in our lives, we are willing to see from a spiritual perspective. We pause, step back from the obstacles or challenge in our lives and sit with it. We listen to the message that's being given. For me, the message I received during the wall experience in my writing was that I was writing a book about trusting my inner spirit, yet I was not trusting my inner spirit to guide me.

Step 2: Under the Wall

I like to think of this step as digging deeper. What's under the wall? What needs to be released so I can move forward? For me, my dream revealed the old beliefs I was holding on to: "I can't. I don't want to. It's too hard." Releasing old beliefs and patterns begins with an awareness of them, followed by a willingness to let them go. During this step of the process, I spent hours each day journaling, getting in touch with my feelings and beliefs, and dialoguing with my inner spirit. The more honest I could be with myself and what I was feeling, the lighter and freer I felt.

Step 3: Around the Wall

In my dream, I took a train and drove a car around the wall. I didn't know where I was going, but I trusted I was being guided to where I needed to go. I've found that frequently when I'm willing to admit I don't know the answer or the direction to take, and I'm willing to humbly ask for guidance, my inner spirit is right there with guidance for me. Often the guidance of our inner spirit doesn't take us on a direct path but leads us in a circuitous journey *around* the wall to exactly where we need to go. When I was experiencing the wall in my writing journey, instead of directly continuing with my manuscript for my book, I would be guided to a writing exercise, a video, or journaling. I later discovered each of these activities to be exactly what I needed at the time in order to learn to write more clearly and effectively.

Step 4: Through the Wall

Moving *through* the wall is being fully present to what is—what we're feeling and experiencing in each moment. If you're feeling resistance, breathe into it. Acknowledge it. Ask, "What do I need to know or do right now?" Sometimes being willing to ask for help is a necessary step to move through resistance. Moving through the wall also involves putting the lessons we've learned into practice—taking the steps we're guided to take, making the decisions we need to make. For me, moving through the wall, when the time was right, meant going back to consistent writing/rewriting of my book.

More often than I'd like to admit, before my wall dream and learning these steps, I would give up or let self-doubt stop me from reaching my desired goal. Learning this four-step process confirmed for me that I don't need to know how to do something or how it will get done. All I need to do is to be willing to trust and take the steps I'm guided to take. Because I was willing to do this, I continued writing my book with clearer focus and intention, I received tools that I've used many times when I've encountered a wall in my life, the process became the inspiration for a Sunday message ("Climbing the Wall: A Parable for Our Time"), and I've been able to share the ideas with anyone who wants to grow through climbing the walls in their lives and trusting their inner spirit more fully. Life is full of surprises when we're willing to trust our inner spirit.

LEARNING TO TRUST

Right now you may be thinking, "I'd love to trust my inner spirit, but I'm not a very trusting person. Can I learn to be more trusting?"

You certainly can! As simple as it seems, the way to learn to trust is by trusting. We learn the principle by practicing it—testing ourselves again and again until we feel more trusting, more in the flow, more confident. We test ourselves by taking a step that we feel guided to take and then noticing how we feel, noticing the results of our actions. This morning, for example, I wasn't feeling in harmony with myself. I felt guided to follow the four-step process for moving through a wall. (The process can be used for tiny walls as well as major challenges in our lives.) I discovered I was putting pressure on myself to be and do what didn't feel right to me. Just being willing to do the process and to acknowledge what I was feeling led me to feeling lighter and freer, helping me move forward with my day.

You might feel guided to take the risk of being authentic and sharing your feelings with a friend with whom you haven't been truthful and find that doing so leads to more open, honest communication between the two of you. You might be guided to take time off from your busy work schedule and go for a walk in the woods, sit on a park bench and watch children play, or simply go outside and enjoy the gentle breeze. And if you do, you might return to your work feeling refreshed and renewed.

ASKING FOR A SIGN

I've found it helpful, especially in the early days of learning to trust my inner spirit, to ask for a sign to verify what I think my inner spirit is telling me. A butterfly is a sign of transformation, but it also reminds me of my mother. She would often give me gifts containing butterfly designs—a pink sparkly pin, a small notepad, a tea cup. A few days after my mother's death, a butterfly appeared on the screen in my bedroom window and simply rested there until I heard the message: *It's time to soar,* a sign to me that my mother was at peace and continuing on her spiritual journey. A cardinal, which my father delighted in watching while he was alive, is a reminder that he's with me in spirit. Often, when I'm feeling alone or experiencing a challenge, I'll see a cardinal or butterfly or I'll receive a card or gift with a cardinal or butterfly design.

Years ago, I was experiencing intense pain and couldn't move my arm and shoulder. I went to an orthopedic surgeon who diagnosed the condition as a frozen shoulder and gave me exercises to do; however, the exercises provided no relief. Frustrated, I talked with my friend Judy, a physical therapist trained in a variety of different healing modalities. Judy agreed to work with me at minimal cost because she considered working with me, as her friend and minister, part of her support of me and the church. (This was a tremendous blessing, as I didn't have health insurance at the time.) Judy worked with me in her home two or three times a week for several months. At one point, when

I wasn't making as much progress as we'd hoped, I wondered whether I should continue the treatments. I felt guided to do so, but I was unsure, so I asked for a sign.

On the way home, driving on a road I'd taken countless times, I saw something I hadn't seen before: a huge sign in front of a church that read, "If you are looking for a sign, you found one!" I continued my physical therapy work with Judy, and after a few months, I regained total mobility and range of motion in my shoulder and arm. I also gained a valuable reminder of the power of signs!

A Trust Walk

Have you ever participated in a trust walk? This is where two people take turns being blindfolded and leading each other on a course. The goal is to create a physically and emotionally safe experience for the partner who's walking without sight. A trust walk can be a powerful experience in learning to trust, but it can also be frightening. As a child, I took part in a trust walk at a friend's backyard party. As my partner—a stranger to me—led me through the obstacles on the walk, I held my breath, hoping he'd keep me safe. I learned then that it takes time to develop trust with another person, and later, that it takes time to learn to trust my inner spirit.

Since the early days of learning to trust my inner spirit, I've used the process of dialoguing with my inner spirit to gain greater clarity and confidence. A few years ago, I discovered a process that took dialoguing with my inner spirit to a deeper level of trust—a virtual trust walk with my inner spirit.

While preparing an inspirational message on "Living a Soulful Life," I was guided to Jodi Chapman's website (jodichapman.com), on which she offered a meditation for reconnecting with your soul.

After a gentle relaxation, we were led to close our eyes, place our hands on our computer keyboard, and respond to a series of questions designed to assist us in connecting to our soul—to type whatever message came to us in that moment. After the meditation, we were invited to reflect on our answers and take them into our hearts. I felt a deep sense of peace and knew that I'd connected with my soul—my inner spirit—on a deep level.

I began to use this exercise when I felt stuck in my writing, needed to clarify what I was feeling, or needed to let go of self-doubt and simply trust my inner spirit. I also created my own questions and listened/typed the responses from my inner spirit. Sometimes when I closed my eyes and began to type, I felt as vulnerable and out of control as a child relying on her partner to keep her safe on a trust walk.

One day when I was concerned about the mistakes I made when typing with my eyes closed, I received this message from my inner spirit:

> *Close your eyes and just type. It lets you feel out of control, but it allows me to lead you. I want you to trust me and feel the lead. Don't take an action until you feel it. Dance with me. Feel in the flow.*

> *When you look down at the typewriter to make sure there are no mistakes, you take yourself out of the flow, like looking at your feet when you are dancing. If you follow the movement of your partner's body and allow yourself to move with your partner, you'll be in the flow. If you trust me to lead you, you'll be in the flow. Mistakes are made when you are not in the flow. Don't you see that when you are in the flow, fewer mistakes are made? And it is okay to make mistakes because that too is part of the process. We can't learn and grow without making mistakes.*

To my amazement, the more I trusted my inner spirit as I was typing with my eyes closed, the fewer typos I made. In this exercise, in ballroom dancing, and in my dance with the Divine, the more I trust, the more I feel in the flow—confident, at ease, and in harmony with myself and with others.

TRUST THE PROCESS

Years ago, my friend Alice gave me advice that has been extremely helpful to me in my journey of following my inner spirit. When things aren't working as we think they should, or when we follow what we believe we were guided to do but don't see the results we expected, or when nothing seems to make sense, *trust the process*. Trust that everything is working as it's meant to, even if we can't see that yet.

It's All About Trust

During the years from 2009–2014, my mother was diagnosed with cognitive impairment, had several falls, and was hospitalized and in rehab for several months at a time. Although she'd lived in her home for ninety-one years and didn't want to leave, the time came when assisted living, and then a skilled nursing facility, seemed like the only viable options. As the only child, I was responsible for making the decisions when she wasn't able to do so. I felt I was following my guidance in making the choices, but the anger she directed at me for placing her in a facility and selling her home (which was necessary to pay for her care) was heartbreaking for me. I questioned whether I'd really followed my guidance. Could I have done it differently? Was there a better way? Through that difficult period, I kept reminding myself to trust the process. It wasn't until a month after her death, while I was at Mariawald Retreat Center for my monthly retreat day, that I received a message that brought me some comfort and a sense of peace in trusting that I had followed the guidance of my inner spirit. On that day, my inner spirit brought me a message from my mother:

> *Your mother wants to thank you for all the time you spent with her and for all the help you gave her. She's sorry that sometimes she wasn't kind to you. She was afraid of letting go, of moving on. Now she sees that there was nothing to fear. She wants you to know how much she loves you. She is watching over you and sending you much more love than you can imagine.*

The more we trust our inner spirit—and learning to trust is an ongoing process—the more Spirit can lead us, and the more flowing and effortless our dance with the Divine becomes.

DANCE STEPS TO PRACTICE TRUSTING YOUR INNER SPIRIT

1. Give thanks in advance.

I have a daily practice of expressing gratitude for the blessings in my life and then expressing gratitude for the blessings I trust that I'll receive. Doing this at the beginning of each day starts the day with a positive focus and sets a positive intention for the day.

Ask yourself, "What do I want to accomplish today?" "How do I want to feel?" "What am I being guided to do or be today?"

Once you set your intentions, preface each one with a "thank you" as an indication of your trust in receiving it. For instance, you might say:

- "Thank you that I write for at least two hours today."
- "Thank you that I feel in the flow of life today."
- "Thank you that I am a peaceful, loving presence today."
- "Thank you that I hear my guidance clearly and follow it completely today."

At the end of the day, take a few minutes to reflect on your intentions for the day. You may be surprised at the way your intentions were realized. Remember to give thanks for the blessings you did receive, and trust that those that are still in process will be realized at the right time and in the right way.

2. Prepare to take an action as guided even if you don't yet see how the desired outcome could possibly come about.

Trust requires action. Following guidance is a sign of trust. If you're unsure that you've heard your guidance correctly or you feel overwhelmed by the guidance you've received, take one small step in the direction of the guidance and observe your feelings. If your intention is to feel greater joy in your life and you suddenly think about a friend you haven't talked to in months, call them (or send a card or an email). If you're inspired to travel to Hawaii and have no idea how you could find the time or the money, visit a travel agent or a travel website and learn about trips to Hawaii, allowing the idea to become a possibility in your mind. Notice how you feel and notice the results of your actions.

3. Expect good to come.

The intention you've set may not come in exactly the way you anticipate, but expect that it will come in the way that's for the highest good of all concerned. Trusting in the right and perfect outcome doesn't mean the outcome looks exactly as we pictured it, but it does mean we receive the essence of what we desire.

For many years, on New Year's Day, I would write a list of my desires or intentions for the year. I would be very specific about what I wanted—an income increase of $1,000 a month or a relationship with a tall, dark, handsome soulmate—and at the end of the year, I'd be disappointed because I didn't receive exactly what I'd asked for. After several years, I received guidance (no doubt when I was willing to hear that guidance), asking me to consider what the essence of what I desired was. When I realized I was feeling more prosperous no matter how much money I had or how much love I already had in my life, I knew that my prayers had been answered.

As you set your intentions, ask yourself, "What do I really want to experience?" "What is truly important to me?" Then expect that blessings will come to you, often in a way you couldn't have imagined.

4. Be aware of obstacles to trusting your inner spirit.

Do you ever find yourself asking, "Why is this happening to me?" or "What if I trust my inner guidance and it doesn't work out the way I think it should?" Or trying to control the outcome after setting your intention? Or feeling resistance in your body? (It takes lots of energy to move against the flow of life.)

If you notice any of these symptoms of not trusting your inner spirit, begin to change your negative thoughts to more positive, trusting ones, such as:

- "Everything is happening exactly as it's meant to."
- "I let go and trust my inner spirit to guide me."
- "I trust in divine timing to bring about the highest and best in the right time and in the right way." (Divine timing and trust are inseparable.)

It's All About Trust

I find that when I change my thoughts to focusing on trust instead of doubt, I feel more relaxed, more at ease, and more trusting.

5. Practice, practice, practice.

Building trust takes patience and practice. The only way we can learn to trust is by trusting. Continue to ask, "What do I need to know?" and "What do I need to do?"—then take the steps you're guided to take. Notice how you feel. Notice the results.

Also, notice when you're holding on to negative thoughts and change them to more positive, trusting thoughts. Practice giving thanks in advance. Practice the dialoguing exercise in the "A Trust Walk" section of this chapter. Practice each day. The more you practice listening and following (the action step taken in trust), the more you'll feel you are dancing in harmony with the Divine.

Chapter 9

One Step at a Time—Moving from Fear to Faith

Can you imagine yourself in a prone position with arms at your sides, legs straight, being lifted high in the air by your dance partner and spun around several times? Talk about fear!

When I agreed to perform a hustle routine with my dance instructor for our Ballroom Break spring showcase, I had no idea I'd be learning the "fish lift" as part of my routine. By this time, I had taken ballroom dance lessons for about five years, performed four or five dance routines (including several lifts), and felt relatively confident in myself as a dancer.

But the fish lift...just the thought of attempting it filled me with terror! (What if my partner dropped me? What if I looked as awkward as I felt? What if I became dizzy or lightheaded?) However, I knew that if I was going to perform the move in the showcase (which I very much wanted to do), I'd have to move from fear to faith—faith that I could learn this lift and even become comfortable performing it, faith in my partner, and faith in myself. Yes, I was afraid, but I was determined to feel the fear and do it anyway.

As I journaled about my fear, my inner spirit advised me: "*You can do this. Take it one step at a time. I will show you how to move from fear to faith. The first step is to be willing.*"

Trusting in the guidance of my inner spirit and of my dance instructor, I moved forward one step at a time. First, I was willing to learn the routine, including the lift. Next, to remedy the dizziness and nausea I felt while spinning in the air, I was inspired to take a ginger capsule, a remedy for motion sickness. (Sometimes our inner spirit can be very practical.) That plus learning how to "spot" (keeping my eyes fixed on a single spot while spinning) and lots of faith allowed me to learn the routine, perform it at the Ballroom Bash that year, and go on to perform it at the Valencia Ballroom in York, Pennsylvania, for the annual Tri-State Ballroom Dance.

In the words of Lao Tzu, "The journey of a thousand miles begins with a single step." That step was my willingness to face my fear. I was then able to move, one step at a time, through the discomfort and resistance I felt; discover new strength and possibilities in myself; and ultimately, perform a dance routine that I hadn't initially thought I could do.

Ballroom dancing has been a fabulous way for me to learn how to take one step at a time. In learning to dance, we begin with basic steps, learn appropriate posture, discover how to move on the dance floor, coordinate the steps with music, and discover patterns…before it all comes together in a dance. And even then, we usually don't know which steps our partner is going to lead, but we follow one step at a time.

Similarly, in our dance with the Divine, we don't know which steps our divine partner is going to lead. We may only see the first step to take, but as we're willing to take that step, our pathway unfolds one step at a time.

When I left my teaching position at West Shore, I had no idea what I was going to do next. I wanted a blueprint for my entire life, but I was given guidance one step at a time. Fortunately, this turned out to be enough. My process involved tutoring and facilitating self-esteem groups for children, starting a business called Integrity (which focused on personal-growth workshops and seminars), and leading a Unity study group, which ultimately led to full-time ministry. Each time I took a step as I was guided, that step led to another and another.

Perfect Choreography

Have you ever tried to figure out how your future would unfold but, as much as you wanted to, couldn't imagine how your desired result would come about?

In the early days of our Unity Church group, when we were exploring the possibility of moving from the Best Western Inn to our own facility, we had no idea how we'd be able to finance our own church building with the small group of people attending the services at the time. One step at a time, we followed what we felt guided to do. We went through the process of incorporation of our ministry and checked out various rental properties in the area, and I applied to the field-licensing program leading to ordination. Then one day I was guided to check the want ads of the Sunday paper, and there was the ad—"Church building for free"—that would lead us to our new church home. We could never have imagined the way in which this sequence of events would bring us our desired result, yet one step at a time, it unfolded for us.

This process is similar to the way a dance routine is created. Even the choreographer doesn't know how the routine will look when it's completed. It unfolds one step at a time. The music is chosen, and beat by beat, measure by measure, the steps unfold. Does this movement, this pattern fit with the music? Is the dancer able to execute this move? Do the movements fit their personality and dance style? The dancer needs to stretch and grow but not be pushed to the breaking point. At the end of the process, a routine has been completed, often surprising both the dancer and the choreographer.

When I look back at the path I traveled to writing this book, I feel sure my divine partner was choreographing every step, one step at a time, in the right and perfect way for me.

When I retired from full-time ministry in 2017, my intention was to take a year off for rest and renewal and to explore what I felt guided to do in the next phase of my life. For many years I'd considered writing a book; my inner spirit had even given me the title. I had written thousands of Sunday messages in the past twenty-five years, but writing a book? I felt intimidated by the task and had no idea how to begin.

In spring 2018, I attended an introductory session on classes being offered at Pathways Institute for Learning, a program for adults fifty-five plus. I heard Sharon O'Brien, an instructor at Dickinson College in Carlisle, Pennsylvania, describe a five-session class she was teaching that semester on memoir and life-writing. I immediately felt a divine nudge to sign up for the class. In the class, I was introduced to the memoir-writing techniques of scene, summary, and musing. I shared, for the first time, stories that would later become part of my book. Best of all, Sharon's encouragement—"I absolutely love the unexpected juxtaposition of spirituality and ballroom dancing"—motivated me to continue writing after the class ended.

In August 2018, while I was perusing ideas for a Sunday message on "Living a Soulful Life," I found Jodi Chapman's website (another divine nudge) and discovered that she and her husband, Dan Teck, were offering a free series of online videos on Soulful Writing. The topics—everything from why I wanted to write a book, to telling stories effectively, to preparing for the inner journey—brought me clarity on the kind of book I wanted to write and why. At that time, Jodi and Dan talked about their yearlong Your Soulful Book program for those who were ready to take the next step in writing their book. The idea excited me, but I didn't feel ready to make this commitment. I did sign up to be on Jodi and Dan's mailing list, however, and the following year, I received an invitation to submit a soulful writing piece for their upcoming book, *365 Messages: The Right Guidance at the Right Time*.

I couldn't resist this divine nudge; after all, writing about divine guidance was my passion. I submitted four pieces, which were accepted for the book. In November 2019, the book was launched, and I was delighted to be a published author. I knew that Jodi and Dan's soulful approach to writing was the path for me, and in December 2019, with a very strong push from my inner spirit, I signed up for their 2020 Your Soulful Book program. The support, knowledge, and step-by-step guidance they offered through this program was instrumental in my completing the book I had been guided to write years before. Had I not been willing to listen to the guidance of my inner spirit, follow my divine nudges, and take the steps I was guided to take, the book you're reading would still be just an idea in my mind.

FEAR RESTRICTS THE FLOW

Have you ever noticed that after you make a major commitment in your life, you begin to encounter fears? "What have I done?" "Do I have what it takes to do this?"

Each step of my journey in writing my book required me to face the fears I felt: Could I really write a book? Would others want to read it? Did I have the courage and stamina to do what I was guided to do?

This feeling of fear can restrict us in many ways. When I'm ballroom dancing, I very quickly notice the effects that fear has on my body. If, instead of being present in the moment, I'm fearing what I might do wrong—make a mistake, miss a cue, or appear ungraceful—these fears keep me from enjoying the dance. I'll feel tension in my body, and it will be difficult for me to follow my partner's lead.

Have you felt this constriction in your body when you're caught up in worry and fear? You may be concerned about any number of things: speaking your truth, getting lost while driving to an unfamiliar place, feeling uncomfortable in a new environment, or facing something you can't control. I've found that if I'm experiencing a lot of fear about a situation in which I'm asking for guidance, I may block the answer, or the fear might cloud the response I receive. Instead of letting my inner spirit lead me, I let fear lead me.

We want to know where we're going to end up *before* we take the first step. But faith doesn't work that way. To dance with the Divine is to step out in faith and let Spirit and life support us. We may see only the first step to take, but as we're willing to take that step, our pathway unfolds one step at a time.

Moving from Fear to Faith

One of my favorite biblical stories, found in Matthew 14:22-33, is the story of Peter walking on water. Jesus' disciples were out on a boat on the Sea of Galilee in a violent storm with gusty winds that sent waves crashing over their small fishing boat. In the midst of their terror, they saw a figure—which they did not initially recognize to be Jesus—walking on the water toward them. As if this weren't frightening enough, Jesus invited Peter to join him. How many of us would accept that invitation? Peter did. He got out of the boat and started walking toward Jesus. Imagine the courage that step required!

When Peter realized what he was doing, he became paralyzed with fear and began to sink. He called out to Jesus, and Jesus immediately reached out his hand and caught him. When they got back into the boat, the winds ceased and the storm subsided.

It's unlikely that any of us will be asked to literally walk on water, but no doubt we all have experienced storms in our lives—times when we felt we were guided to take steps that we were afraid to take. Feeling fear is a natural reaction when we're asked to step out of our comfort zone into the unknown.

What stands out for me in the story of Peter walking on water is that as soon as he asked for help, assistance was given *immediately*. He took a step in faith, and when he began to doubt himself and ask for help, it was there, no questions asked. Just as Jesus was there for Peter, our inner spirit is there for us when we ask for help.

One Step at a Time—Moving from Fear to Faith

In 2015, after countless repairs to our slate roof at our hundred-year-old church building, our congregation faced the prospect of replacing a large part of the irreparably damaged roof. As our council met to discuss our options and the apparent lack of money to pay for the roof, we expressed our fears and doubts about being able to come up with the money in time to complete the roof before winter.

In Unity, we have a catchphrase: "In any situation, go to God first." Like Peter, we asked for help, for guidance. I invited each council member to commit to affirming daily this truth for our ministry: "Divine love is doing its perfect work in this situation now. We are clearly guided to the steps that are ours to take. We trust in the right and perfect outcome. Thank you, God." Then each member was asked to listen to the guidance of their own inner spirit. Just affirming those words helped us feel a sense of calm and trust in the process.

Within a few days of taking this first step, Linda, one of our council members, volunteered to procure estimates from several contractors in the area. Replacing a slate roof was very expensive, several of the contractors couldn't do the work within the requested time frame, and none of the options felt right to us. Then, while browsing lists of contractors online, Linda was drawn to a company run by an Amish gentleman in the area. When he visited our church, Linda and I were impressed with his sincere interest in the church and his commitment to be of service to us. He suggested an option we hadn't considered—a shingled roof instead of slate, which would be less expensive and extremely durable. Although he couldn't personally provide that option, as his specialty was slate roofing, he was able to subcontract with another company to complete the work for us. Throughout the process, this gentleman was actively involved in making sure we were satisfied with the work completed.

We felt that we were divinely guided in finding the right person to lead us in our roof replacement. Next, another council member and her partner offered a $10,000 interest-free, one-year loan—the amount we needed in addition to our savings—and the promise that whatever wasn't paid off in one year would be given to the church as a gift. Another council member established a fundraiser to raise the amount needed to pay back the loan. The money was raised by the end of the year, and we had a beautiful new roof!

We took a first step in faith toward our goal, and although we could not foresee the outcome at that point, one step led to another, and the goal was reached.

STEPPING OUT OF THE BOAT

Are there areas of your life where you, like Peter or like the Unity of Palmyra council, are feeling a divine nudge to step out of the boat, out of your comfort zone? To try something you've never tried before? To step out of the familiar routine of your life? To face a fear?

When we follow our inner spirit, at some point we'll be called to step out of our comfort zones, which requires courage and vulnerability. We never know when the opportunity to test ourselves will occur. For me, the chance to step out of my comfort zone and into my vulnerability happened at a retreat with my soulful book group.

It's a Sunday morning in October, and I—dressed in my blue-and-white-flowered silky pajamas—am attending, with my fellow writers at the Your Soulful Book virtual retreat, a "pajama party" session on "Writing Through Your Vulnerability." As instructed, I've prepared a piece to share from my book. I've taken great care in choosing a piece that I feel is well written, has lots of details, creates a scene for the reader, and makes me feel slightly uncomfortable to read. (Just the right amount of vulnerability!) But as I'm waiting for my turn to share my story, I feel a nudge from my inner spirit: "*Share the other piece. The one about the conflict at Unity of Palmyra. The one that almost caused you to leave your ministry.*"

"Oh, no," I think. "I can't share that. It isn't finished. It has notes scribbled all over it." (Why I even considered sharing this piece, I don't know. When I tried to rewrite it a few days earlier, I couldn't find the words to describe what I wanted to say, so I put it in my unfinished folder to be perused sometime in the future.)

"*Share that piece,*" I hear again.

One of my intentions at this retreat is to allow myself to be vulnerable. And what could be more vulnerable than reading a piece that's unfinished, certainly not good enough to be shared? What will people think? (That I'm a bad writer? That I've come unprepared?)

Sometimes when we resist the voice of our inner spirit, it becomes louder; the nudge becomes stronger. Almost as if I feel a hand pushing gently on my back, I open my mouth to speak to the group: "I think the piece I planned to share is not the one I need to share." (By speaking the words out loud, I know I've committed myself to sharing the writing about my ministry.)

During the five-minute break, I find the piece I am to share, quickly look over it, knowing it's too late to change anything about it. I have to share it, warts and all. When it's my turn to share, I preface my reading with disclaimers: "I know this isn't finished. It's only a first draft. I don't even know if I can read it; there are so many notes scribbled all over the paper."

I take a few deep breaths and begin to read…

When I finish, I hold my breath, waiting for the feedback. (I know it will be loving, as this is a loving, supportive group, yet I still feel very vulnerable.) I receive suggestions as to how to dig deeper into the story, and one comment that touches my heart: "I can see the kind of person you are from what you wrote."

This simple statement, spoken by a woman I barely knew, validated my integrity in the conflict at my ministry. These words would become a catalyst for me to explore and heal the pain of self-doubt hidden in the story I was guided to share.

Sometimes our inner spirit wants us to step out of our comfort zone, honor our intentions, and trust that there's a reason to do what we're guided to do, even when we don't know what that reason is. In being willing to trust my inner spirit's guidance, I felt empowered to move through my vulnerability, I gained helpful suggestions for rewriting my piece, and I received an unexpected gift that brought healing for me.

IN A FOG

Sometimes in our dance with the Divine, we're so in harmony with our inner spirit that we don't need to ask for guidance; we just know what step to take. Other times, we feel like we're in a fog and can't see the next step. We feel alone in the dance. This was my experience at the eight-day silent retreat at the Jesuit Community Center in Wernersville, where each day I was guided to a place that represented what I needed to learn that day. I was pondering not only what I'd do that day, but what I'd do next in my life. I was standing on a balcony overlooking the retreat center grounds, seeing thick fog in some areas, clear sky in others. I wrote in my journal:

> As I gaze at the fog, I see a mirror for where I am in my life right now. In some areas of my life, I feel I have received clear guidance, and other areas are foggy. In my mind, I hear the words to the song "In His Time," and I know I am being told that all things will be clear to me in perfect divine timing. In the

> meantime, I can do what I know to do right now and wait for the fog to clear and greater clarity to come. Or I can ask, "What am I to do in the meantime?" I know that out there somewhere, beyond where I can see, is the future—the unknown—and at the right time, it will be revealed.

As the ancient Chinese philosopher Lao Tzu so eloquently asks, "Do you have the patience to wait until the mud settles and the water is clear?" Sometimes life presents us with several paths, and the way is not clearly defined. Sometimes we must walk a bit on each path to see where it leads, to know whether it's the right path for us. And sometimes a path dead-ends. We know we can go no further on that path, so we choose another.

In the transitional period moving from teaching at West Shore to full-time ministry, I walked several paths for a while. I taught self-esteem classes and facilitated groups for children and adults. I tutored children in developing reading skills. I began a business, Integrity, which focused on personal-growth classes and support groups. I started a Unity study group. Over time, and partly because I no longer maintained my contact base from my teaching days, my tutoring and self-esteem classes for children were no longer attracting participants.

I realized this was a transitional step that moved me from full-time teaching to my work in ministry. I enjoyed the classes and support groups I facilitated through Integrity, but as our church group grew and set the intention to be a full-time ministry, my path veered in a different direction. Although I didn't know it at the time, each path was a step leading to ministry.

One Step at a Time—Moving from Fear to Faith

Sometimes we think we know what step we're meant to take, but we aren't ready to take it. When you read the story of Peter walking on water, do you ever wonder why Jesus didn't invite the other disciples, who were also sitting in the boat during that storm at sea, to come walk on the water? Why did he only invite Peter? I imagine that Jesus knew his disciples well enough to know which one was ready to take that step in faith. Also, Peter was the only disciple who responded when he saw Jesus coming toward them. Peter asked Jesus to command him to come to him on the water. He indicated that he was ready to take that step out of the boat and into the unknown. Jesus didn't force anyone to take that step until they were ready. Being ready was important.

In most of the major decisions I've made in my life, there was a period of time between my having a vision of my goal and actually reaching the goal, a time when I didn't feel ready to move forward.

At a retreat at Stella Maris Retreat Center in Long Branch, New Jersey, two years before I retired, I was thinking about how and when I would leave my ministry. I was considering telling my council members at Unity of Palmyra of my plans to leave, even though at that point I didn't know when that time would come. I planned on asking them to be part of the process of preparing our ministry for the time when I would no longer be their minister. I shared this plan with my spiritual director at Stella Maris during one of our meetings and felt good about the choice. That evening, though, I felt a tremendous sense of sadness and loss at the thought of leaving my ministry. I asked for a sign that my choice was the right one. The next day as I was sitting on a bench overlooking the ocean and feeling a gentle breeze blowing my hair, I read these words from the book *When the Heart Waits* by Sue Monk Kidd:

> When it comes to letting go, we have to arrive at a moment of genuine readiness. We need to quit forcing things and allow God to draw to us our moment of readiness.

These words resonated with me. Was this the sign that I was asking for? Was it telling me that I knew the time of leaving Unity of Palmyra was coming, that I had taken steps already to prepare for the time when I'd leave, that I didn't have to force the process, that I could let it unfold as the words of Sue Monk Kidd expressed so well?

As I sat in the silence and listened, I heard these simple but powerful words: "*You don't have to leave until you are ready!*" I felt such a sense of relief and comfort in hearing these words. In that moment, I knew that the time would come when I'd be ready. In the meantime, I'd be guided on the steps to take, one step at a time.

Do You Have the Courage?

At some point in our dance with the Divine, the guidance is clear, we are ready—though not entirely without fear—and it's time to move out of our comfort zone and step forward into the new, the unknown, the possibility. Yet we still sometimes get stuck in the thinking stage and resist moving forward. This can happen in all areas of life—including ballroom dance. For instance, during one of my sessions at Ballroom Break dance studio, an instructor noticed my hesitation in moving forward in a step called the hip twist, a move requiring quick and decisive movement. She told my instructor, "Tell Julie to just go." When I stopped thinking about and analyzing the movement and finally moved forward with confidence, I was on my way.

One of my favorite sayings is "A ship in harbor is safe, but that is not what ships are built for" (from John A. Shedd's 1928 collection of sayings, *Salt from My Attic*). This reminds me of the importance of taking steps forward. These words have been a guide for me when I feel myself getting in a rut, afraid to move out of my comfort zone even when I know that it's time to move forward. In our dance with the Divine, there comes a time when we each have to leave the harbor and take the steps we're guided to take, no matter how difficult, no matter how much these steps don't seem to make sense to our logical minds. We have to move from fear to faith.

Dance Steps for Moving from Fear to Faith

1. Pause, slow down, and go within.

In the words of a student in one of my Trusting Your Inner Spirit classes, "When I'm in a situation of heightened anxiety or tension, I feel calmer when I slow down." If you're experiencing anxiety or fear, take a few minutes to pause, slow down, close your eyes if possible, and take a few deep breaths. Focus on a calming thought, such as:

- "I have all the time I need."
- "I am calm and at ease."
- "I can do this."

The act of consciously breathing and focusing on a calming thought allows our fear to dissipate and helps us connect with our inner spirit and see from a clearer perspective.

2. Face the fear.

Because the feeling of fear is uncomfortable to most of us, we try to push it aside, ignore it, or hide it from ourselves and others. Instead, when you feel fear, breathe into it and acknowledge what you're feeling, even if only to yourself—thinking, "I'm feeling afraid right now," rather than "I shouldn't feel afraid" or "There's nothing to be afraid of." As best as you can, identify the fear. Asking "What exactly am I afraid of?" provides space for you to explore the fear and narrow it down to a specific and manageable fear. Accept fear as part of your growth. We all experience fear when we step out of our comfort zones or attempt a new skill or activity. Fear is often the cutting edge, moving you out of a rut and into greater creativity or courage.

3. Focus on the goal or desired outcome.

What do you want to experience? What goal are you moving toward? Focus on what you want to experience instead of imagining the worst-case scenario. Once you've identified your desired outcome, feed that intention with positive attention through your thoughts. Use affirmations such as:

- "I can do this."
- "I can handle this."
- "I have all the support I need to move through this fear."

4. Take a small step in the direction of the desired outcome.

If you aren't sure what step to take, ask yourself, "If there were no fear, what would I do?" I'm always amazed at the answers I receive when I ask this question, which really gets to the heart of the matter. Once when I was pondering my choices about leaving ministry and when to tell my congregation, I asked this question, and the answer came immediately: "*I'd wait until my guidance is absolutely clear. I'd stop trying to figure out the solution and trust*

Spirit to guide me in the moment as to what to say and what to do."

Since taking a step toward the desired goal or outcome—no matter how small that step seems to be—builds trust, taking a step is essential in moving forward. Ask, "What small step am I willing to take right now?" Think of a step that is small and manageable enough that it causes little or no fear in this moment, then take that step—not tomorrow, not a week from now, but right now!

5. Keep moving forward one step at a time.

As you take each step, experience positive results, and see that everything you need is provided, you gain confidence and trust to keep on going. As you continue, keep asking your inner sprit for guidance: "What's the next step for me to take?"

To ensure you're listening to the voice of your inner spirit and not your fear, tune in to your body. Does the choice you're considering make you feel more open and expansive or more shut down and restricted? Faith, the voice of our inner spirit, expands; fear contracts. Tune in to your feelings. Ask yourself, "Does this step feel right to me? Do I feel peaceful, excited, and joyful in considering this step?" If no step feels right in this moment, another option may appear in time. Sometimes the step to take is to wait and listen.

Sometimes we need to ask for support as we continue to move forward. We definitely need to move at our own pace. And sometimes, as we keep moving forward, we find that our goal changes. The process of moving from fear to faith changes us, one step at a time, and expands our idea of what's possible in ways that we couldn't have imagined when we began the journey. When we commit to moving ahead and facing our fears, the power of faith takes over. It becomes a bridge moving us from fear to our desired outcome or goal.

When I'm feeling a bit hesitant to take the steps from fear to faith, I find it helpful to do a visualization that I call "The Bridge of Faith":

> Imagine something you desire to experience in your life—something you may feel called to do or be, even though you don't know how to bring it into your life or how it would even be possible. (The more impossible it seems, the more likely your inner spirit is inspiring you with this desire.) Next, in your mind's eye, see what's keeping you from experiencing the fulfillment of this desire. What fear is holding you back?
>
> Imagine before you a bridge connecting you and your desire. The only thing holding you back is your fear. Are you willing to face that fear and take one step in faith onto the bridge? Yes, it may require courage; you may not think you can take that first step. But you can. See yourself affirming, "I can do this. I have everything I need inside myself to take the first step."
>
> Take a deep breath and see yourself taking that first step onto the bridge. Feel the excitement and joy as your feet are firmly planted on the bridge. And now see yourself taking another step—and another and another—your confidence and trust growing as you continue on this journey. Allow

yourself to go as far as you're ready to go across this bridge right now. Maybe you'll reach the other side today or maybe tomorrow—whenever the time is right. You're free to move at your own pace. With every step you take, you move closer to your heart's desire. Continue to take those steps—one step at a time!

Chapter 10

Keep On Keeping On

You have to love dancing to stick to it....Dancing gives you nothing but that single fleeting moment when you feel alive.

– Merce Cunningham

It takes persistence to become an accomplished, confident ballroom dancer. Those who perform dance routines or enter competitive ballroom dancing spend hours each day or each week practicing. Although I have never competed, I have performed at least ten dance routines over the years. The routines, which are usually about two and a half minutes long, require hours and hours of preparation in order for them to go smoothly. Even to look and feel good at social dances or to maintain a moderate level of proficiency in dancing requires ongoing practice.

Sometimes persistence for me means doing a step over and over again until I want to scream, "Enough already!" Sometimes persistence involves going back to steps or patterns I thought I mastered months or even years ago, only to discover that I've forgotten how to do them. In fact, sometimes when my instructor mentions one of these steps, it looks so foreign to me that I ask, "Are you sure I learned that one?" Then it's practice and more practice until I recall, "Oh, yes, I do remember this step. It's beginning to look familiar!"

Lessons to Learn

Dancing with the Divine can be like this. On our spiritual journey, we learn lessons unique to our self-development. You may have learned lessons through illness or loss—to appreciate each day or to make time for the people in your life who are important to you. Through challenges or conflicts in your life, you may have discovered that you have inner strength and courage you didn't know you had. You may have learned to value yourself, to take responsibility for your needs, to follow your heart, to recognize and share your talents and skills. There are countless lessons we may learn in this lifetime. I believe we come into our life experience with particular lessons to learn. As in dancing, sometimes we think we've learned the lessons, only to discover that they reappear in some other form later in our lives. Frequently,

Keep On Keeping On

we're surprised to find the same lessons back again: "Oh, I thought I learned that lesson years ago, and now here it is again!"

As I was writing this book, I looked back at my journals over the years and noticed the same lessons appearing over and over again in different situations. My lessons often centered around self-worth, being true to myself, and most often (not surprisingly since I see it as the guiding principle in my life), trusting my inner spirit. Over the years, I've learned that this is a natural process, a type of spiral learning. At different stages of our growth, we learn the lessons at a deeper level.

Several years after I left my teaching position and was exploring different options for my life, I was becoming frustrated. I felt that if there were lessons for me to learn in this experience, I was ready to learn them so I could move on. But my inner spirit had other ideas about this:

> *You remain at any one level until you learn the lessons there—then you move on. This isn't a punishment but an opportunity. Just as a bird can't fly until it is physically able, you can't soar to a higher level until you've learned the lessons here. To do so would be detrimental to you. It seems unfair to you now. You are tired and frustrated, but all really is in divine order. You are preparing to soar, and when the time is right, soar you will! Keep on keeping on!*

It was years before I felt that I was soaring, but during this unsettling time in my life, I did learn valuable lessons—persistence, trust, following the lead of my inner spirit, taking one step at a time—which were preparation for moving forward in my life as a minister, spiritual teacher, and dancer with the Divine.

If you're wondering why you're attracting the same lessons over and over again, you may find comfort, as I did, in the words of Pema Chödrön, an American Tibetan Buddhist teacher: "Nothing ever goes away until it teaches us what we need to know."

STANDING ON THE BATTLEFIELD

Have there been times in your life when you wanted to quit? When you felt overwhelmed? When your life didn't seem to be going the way you thought it should?

When we commit to following our inner spirit, sometimes our powers of determination and persistence are severely tested. Such was the case for me after I'd been serving as minister at Unity of Palmyra for twelve years.

"I feel like I'm standing on the battlefield and I don't know who the enemy is." I wrote these words in my journal after our annual meeting at Unity of Palmyra in October 2014—harsh words for a minister to describe her feelings about her congregation and her role as minister! This was undoubtedly the lowest point in my years of ministry.

In the past year, several council members had accused me of being controlling, causing "good people" to leave the church, and disregarding the wishes of the congregation. They sent emails to me and to members of the congregation describing my offenses. One of them even said I'd been acting like a cult leader!

How had we come to this place of disharmony? In the years I'd served as minister, I'd felt respected and loved by members of my congregation. I'd tried to be open and honest, willing and eager to talk with congregants whenever there were differences of opinion.

Later, I would understand, through my own reflections and by talking with my friend and regional church consultant, that just as I had expectations for myself, members of my congregation had expectations for me as their minister. When I disappointed them, didn't respond as they'd hoped, or failed to understand what they wanted and needed, they often grew resentful or angry. When these feelings were not acknowledged and discussed between us, they continued to build until conflict exploded in our ministry.

In that moment of feeling as if I were standing on a battlefield, however, I didn't understand what was happening. I didn't know who I could trust. I felt angry, hurt, betrayed, and absolutely alone. My old doubts of feeling unworthy to be a minister resurfaced. Wasn't a minister supposed to be perfect?

With every fiber of my being, I wanted to quit. I considered early retirement. I considered leaving my ministry and becoming a hospice chaplain. I considered applying to another ministry. Disheartened and distraught, I didn't think anyone or anything could persuade me to change my mind, but something did. What changed my mind?

I knew—deep inside myself—that I *did* know who I could trust. I could trust my inner spirit to guide me. In addition, I was blessed to receive the emotional support I needed from Pat, my regional church consultant.

Through many discussions with Pat and hours of dialoguing with my inner spirit, I knew that, difficult as it might be for me to stay, my leaving the church would not only be a mistake for me but for the congregation as well—leaving in conflict could very well be the end of the church. My inner spirit assured me that if I was willing to persist, ultimately there would be a gift for me and for the church. I needed to stay and keep on keeping on. And so I did.

I was determined to learn and grow through the challenges I faced. Step by step, I followed my guidance. I met with council members and congregants who were willing to talk with me. I listened to their concerns (and sometimes accusations) with as much calm and caring as I could muster. I tried to reassure congregants who were frightened and confused. I accepted responsibility for times when I could have responded in a more thoughtful, caring way. I continued to take care of the daily business of the church. I spent time each day journaling my feelings of fear, doubt, and hurt. I spent hours listening to the voice of my inner spirit, which was always there for me. I kept believing that there would be a positive outcome for me and for the church, even though I couldn't yet see how that would unfold.

Keep On Keeping On

After months of conflict, several council members, who felt that their ideas and concerns weren't in harmony with the church as a whole, resigned their positions and decided to leave the church. It's always sad for a congregation to lose members, especially as a result of conflict. However, in the next few months, out of the ashes came a new beginning for our ministry. Six new people came forward to serve on the council—people who were committed to serving, to healing, to moving our ministry forward. My inner spirit was right. As is most often true in a challenge, there is a gift—and the bigger the challenge, the greater the gift. With this new council, I felt a sense of peace and a harmony of purpose that I hadn't felt in many years. Without the constant disagreements and accusations our former council faced, we were able to make choices for new programs, classes, and activities that helped breathe new life and energy into our ministry.

After weathering the storm together, our congregation felt a renewed sense of unity and purpose. We were able to create what I considered to be two of the most prosperous, supportive, and cohesive years of our ministry. When I did retire from Unity of Palmyra two years later, all of us were stronger and more able to move forward with courage and strength.

Through this experience and other challenges throughout my life, I've learned that we always have a choice: quit or keep on keeping on. A breakthrough—a completion, a resolution, a transformation—comes *after* the commitment to keep on keeping on.

Watching *Dancing with the Stars*, I've often seen contestants feeling weary, bruised, frustrated, and discouraged after weeks of intense practice, ready to quit. Time and again, though, through the encouragement, guidance, and support of their professional partners, they've kept on dancing, often moving through their challenges to perform a breakthrough dance—a dance that far exceeded the passion, skills, and confidence they had previously exhibited.

Likewise, how many times in my own ballroom dancing did I think about quitting when I couldn't master a pattern or step I'd practiced over and over again for a routine, when I was afraid I'd never look good enough on the dance floor? But, like the *Dancing with the Stars* contestants, through the patience and encouragement of my dance instructor, I kept on until I broke through the resistance and fear to master the step, perform the routine, and feel more confident as a dancer.

In the conflict at Unity of Palmyra, I knew I wanted to leave ministry when I was *guided* to leave, not because I was pushed out by those who no longer wanted me there, not because the situation was too difficult, not because I felt I wasn't good enough. Whatever the outcome, I chose to let my inner spirit lead me—to keep on listening, trusting, and following my inner spirit's guidance. In the process, I broke through fear and doubt about my abilities as a minister; realized that with the guidance of my inner spirit, I could get through any challenge life might bring me; and felt empowered to move forward to whatever the future would bring.

Keep On Keeping On

Although you may not have felt as if you were standing on a battlefield and not knowing who the enemy is in an outer situation in your life, you may have felt as if you were standing on a battlefield inside yourself. Inner battles can test our powers of persistence as much as outer ones.

Throughout my journey in learning to follow my inner spirit, my inner battle has been between following the rules and expectations of others or trusting and following my inner spirit. Just when I think I've mastered the art of trusting my inner spirit, I find that my perceptions are tested.

When I'm learning something new or feeling insecure, I tend to go to my default mode of operation: following the rules or expectations of others. This happened when I began writing this book. Because writing a book was a new venture for me, I often felt uncertain of how to express myself in the best possible way or whether I should include a particular paragraph or page I'd written. I was afraid I'd make a mistake, do it wrong, or embarrass myself by my poor quality of writing. Each time I had a question about my writing, I'd spend hours searching for the answers in workbooks from my Your Soulful Book program or on videos or blogs by other writers. Although getting this information was often very beneficial for me, it also became overwhelming or confusing, as there were so many options. Eventually, I had to make a decision as to which option I'd choose. Then, often as a last resort, I'd ask and receive guidance from my inner spirit. I could have saved lots of time and energy if I'd asked my inner spirit *first* and then gone to the outer information I was guided to use.

Like Lyn, a student in one of my classes, your inner battle may involve letting go of negative thoughts or getting stuck in the past:

> What's most difficult for me about recognizing, listening to, and following my inner spirit is getting out of my head and not listening to negative, repetitive thoughts. Also getting stuck in the past. The past is no longer. I find learning from the past to be valuable, but the errors or mistakes—regardless of my insightful concept about them—can strike fear in me. Fear stops me. Once I realize what I am doing, then I just get quiet and go within.
> I wait too long to do it!

I'm sure most of us can identify with Lyn's final statement: "I wait too long to do it!" Haven't we all asked ourselves on our journey in learning to listen to our inner spirit, "Why did it take me so long to simply get quiet and listen?"

Whatever your battlefield is, the first step in learning to trust your inner spirit, as Lyn stated, is becoming aware. What old habit do you return to in times of stress, fear, or doubt? Once you recognize your default method, then you have a choice: to continue with what no longer works for you or to choose a new way—the way of listening to and following your inner spirit.

This process of catching yourself in old patterns of behavior and choosing new ways of responding takes determination and persistence, but I believe that the results are worth it. When you choose to follow your inner spirit, you feel a sense of calm, confidence, and ease.

WHAT EXACTLY IS PERSISTENCE?

Usually we think of persistence as a positive quality. Persistent people are determined, confident, and courageous. They have a strong sense of purpose and are often thought of as people who succeed, who don't give up or let doubts and fears stop them from doing what they want to do or feel guided to do.

But can we be too persistent? Most of us have probably experienced someone who tried to fix us, convince us to do something that didn't feel right to us, or change our mind to be more in harmony with their thinking. Maybe we've been that person on occasion.

I sometimes find myself pushing too hard, holding on to a rigid idea of how it *should* be. (There's that word again—always a red flag for me—a sign that I'm following my fears rather than my inner spirit.)

Years ago, I was in a relationship that wasn't working for me. I tried to make the situation and the other person be the way I thought they *should* be, but this just made the relationship feel like a constant battle. Then one morning I heard my inner spirit say, *"Why are you trying so hard to make this relationship work when there is someone so much better for you?"* Why indeed?

What persistence comes down to for me is: What's driving me? Is persistence a way of controlling, is it fear-driven, or am I guided by a sense of purpose, by the wisdom of my inner spirit?

When my inner spirit is the one leading me, I'll be guided one step at a time without needing to control, force, or make something happen. When my inner spirit is guiding me, I'll be able to keep focused and unwavering in spite of outer appearances. I'll be able to stay the course and act courageously.

DO WE REALLY NEED PERSISTENCE?

In our dance with the Divine, persistence is essential in learning to recognize, listen to, trust, and follow our inner spirit. Let's explore these steps one at a time.

It takes persistence to learn to recognize the voice of our inner spirit.

There are so many voices competing for our attention. On the outside, there are voices of our parents, peers, authority figures, and the media. Each is telling us what's expected of us, suggesting the attitudes and beliefs we ought to hold. Sometimes these suggestions are positive and life affirming, but at times, they're based on negative ideas and limiting beliefs. These voices can speak loudly and forcefully and are often difficult to ignore. Sometimes these voices are internalized as inner critics, which can be judgmental, condescending, and so powerfully ingrained in us that it's challenging to quiet them. They're the voices that say,

"Who do you think you are to speak in front of hundreds of people?" "What makes you think you have the skills to apply for that job you've been thinking about?" "You never stick to anything; what makes you think this time will be different?"

In contrast to these negative voices, our inner spirit is wise, loving, and kind. It wants the best for us. It reminds us of what we know deep inside ourselves. We often hear our inner voice and have an aha sensation; the message we receive feels right to us. The inner spirit seeks peace, not conflict. It speaks to us in a way that's natural for us to receive. It may speak to us mentally, through persistent thoughts, images, and ideas. It may speak to us emotionally, through our feelings. We may feel excitement, peace, or joy; we may perceive how another person feels without being told; we may have a gut feeling that tells us what guidance is right for us. It may speak to us kinesthetically, through physical sensations such as a pain in the neck, a headache, chills, feeling comfortable or uncomfortable, or feeling energy in our bodies.

The voice of our inner spirit can be persistent because what it's saying is so important for us to hear. Like a loving friend, it will remind us over and over again until we're ready and willing to listen. Many of the messages I've received, especially the ones that asked me to move way beyond my comfort zone, have been repeated many times until I felt ready and willing to listen. Leaving my teaching position without knowing what I'd do next, beginning the path to becoming an ordained minister, retiring from ministry, and writing my book all required numerous messages before I was ready to take the steps I was guided to take.

Jeff, a student in one of my Trusting Your Inner Spirit classes, describes his process of moving from hearing the outer voices vying for his attention to recognizing the voice of his inner spirit:

> What's difficult for me in recognizing the voice of my inner spirit is learning to change my many conditioned responses to life challenges and drama. I have to be conscious and intentional about recognizing and pausing before I react to life situations. I frequently do so by saying, "I don't know what this means." This creates the space to ask and listen. This is an ongoing challenge, as it's so easy to go unconscious and react from my fearful and defensive self. But experience has taught me that the choice is clear—peace from inner guidance or stress and strain from my ego.

It takes persistence to learn to listen to our inner spirit.

In contrast to our inner critic and the negative voices we may hear, our inner spirit speaks only as loudly as our willingness to listen. *Conversations with God* by Neale Donald Walsh, an insightful and thought-provoking book, was, I believe, one of the first mass-market publications to actually record someone's conversations with Spirit. Many people found it amazing that God—Spirit, our inner spirit—actually talked with a human being. But the truth is, each one of us has access to Spirit—twenty-four hours a day, seven days a week, 365 days a year—at any time we're willing to listen.

When we're first learning to listen and to recognize the voice of Spirit, it's essential to schedule time to pause, slow down, and actively listen—a time when we pause from the busyness of our daily lives and allow ourselves to sit in silence. Initially, pausing from the busyness of life may consist of a few minutes in the morning or evening, a quiet time of reflection during a walk in nature, or listening to relaxing, comforting music and letting go of the distractions of the day. If we're not in the habit of listening to or recognizing the voice of our inner spirit speaking to us, this may require persistence until we're able to quiet our minds enough to actually hear the voice within us. Over time, and with a commitment to listening to our inner spirit, we'll find that we hear our inner spirit's guidance even when we're going through our daily routine. The more we take time to listen and follow the guidance we receive, the more we'll want to spend time in silence to communicate with our inner spirit at an even deeper level.

It takes persistence to learn to trust our inner spirit.

Because our inner spirit often speaks in a more gentle, loving language than we're accustomed to, we may not trust it at first. We might ask, "Is this for real?" "Can this affirming, supportive message really be for me?" Hearing the voice of our inner spirit can also be uncomfortable for us, as it may lead us to make choices or take steps that move us to face fears, stretch beyond our comfort zones, and grow in ways we hadn't anticipated. Sometimes it may give us guidance that seems illogical. ("You want me to do *what?* Leave my teaching job of eighteen years without knowing what I'm going to do next?")

We learn to trust our inner spirit by taking one step at a time—as small a step as we need to take—and noticing how we feel when we follow the guidance we're given. When we follow our inner spirit, we may feel in the flow of life. We may experience greater peace of mind, joy, energy, or clarity. We may find ourselves becoming more creative, able to make decisions more easily, feeling a greater sense of purpose and direction. We may experience more synchronicities (meaningful coincidences). But when we don't follow our inner spirit, we may feel out of harmony with ourselves—frustrated, anxious, fearful, confused. When we discover the positive effects of following our inner spirit, it's an incentive to keep on listening and following. Just as in any relationship, trust builds over time.

Linda, another student in one of my classes, describes her process of learning to trust her inner spirit with this analogy:

> Learning to trust your inner spirit is like learning to ride a bike. You fall a lot! When I got my first bike, my dad wouldn't put training wheels on the bike. He told me I had to learn to ride without them. I tried and tried, but I couldn't stay up. I decided to put my bike in the shed and forget about it. But when someone riding a bike passed my house, I'd watch closely to see how it was done. After some time, I decided to try riding again. To my surprise, I was able to stay up. Learning to trust my inner spirit is much the same for me. I watch others whom I feel are clearly guided by their inner spirit, and I try to learn from them. (I recognize them by their ability to live with authenticity and integrity.) I've learned that taking time to quiet myself, listen

to my inner spirit's wisdom, and act as guided is the key to learning to trust my inner spirit.

It takes persistence to learn to follow our inner spirit.

"You know what to do—now do it!" When I was student teaching in preparation for my teaching career, my mentor used this statement with the children. This proclamation had a lasting effect on me, as I still think about it almost fifty years later! It seems to apply to following our inner spirit. The guidance is clear—now follow it! Sounds straightforward and effortless, doesn't it? Or does it?

As a ballroom dancer, I've seen that there's often a gap between knowing what to do and doing it. I've watched my dance instructor demonstrate a new step in the rumba or cha-cha and thought, "That looks easy enough; I can do that," only to find that executing the step required more concentration, coordination, and effort than I expected.

In following our inner spirit, whether we're beginners or have been practicing for many years, there are times when our guidance appears to be perfectly clear yet we hesitate to follow it or we find that following it requires more trust, courage, or effort than we anticipated. For instance, I've often found it challenging to follow my inner spirit's guidance about my physical health. Sometimes I'm afraid that if I dare to trust my own inner knowing rather than following my doctor's advice, I'll irreparably damage my body. I had the opportunity to challenge this belief several years ago during my annual mammogram.

Following my mammogram, a "spot" appeared on the X-ray. I was told that it most likely was a calcium deposit and that on a scale from one to ten, this spot appeared to be in the lowest risk category. However, the radiologist suggested I have a biopsy. During that procedure, a metal piece would be placed at the spot so that it could be identified in future mammograms. This didn't feel right to me, so I indicated that I wanted to think about it and discuss it with my family physician. My guidance was that it wasn't a problem and I didn't need to have the procedure at that time. I hesitated. I clearly heard the voice of my inner spirit, but following it felt like a risk I didn't know if I was willing to take.

The radiologist was persistent in trying to persuade me to do the procedure, but my guidance was even more persistent. I heard over and over again, *"No. You don't need to have this procedure."* I chose to follow my guidance.

In the next months, during my times of meditation, I sent love and light to my body. I affirmed healing of anything that needed to be healed. I began to feel more confident that I'd made the right choice in not having the procedure.

A year later, when I scheduled my yearly mammogram, I have to admit, I felt a bit of apprehension. What if I'd been wrong? What if the spot was still there or had grown? The mammogram was clear; there was no sign of a spot or any abnormality. I believe that my guidance was correct and prevented me from having an unnecessary procedure.

Although I'm not advocating ignoring medical advice, I am advocating being aware of what your body, mind, and emotions are telling you. Listening to your body, mind, and emotions is an important part of recognizing the voice of your inner spirit and trusting its guidance. Sometimes the outer voices of authority speak louder than the voice of our inner spirit, and it takes courage to follow what we know to be true.

What keeps you from knowing what to do and doing it? The strong pull of outer authority, the fear of making a mistake, the concern of disappointing others, or the guilt of putting ourselves first often takes priority over following our inner spirit's guidance.

If you're willing to persist in identifying your barriers to following guidance and exploring alternative choices, you will have taken important steps in learning to trust and follow your inner spirit.

DANCE STEPS FOR PRACTICING PERSISTENCE

1. Set a clear intention/goal/vision.

Clarity on our dance with the Divine comes from within. Persist in a daily practice of taking time to be still, to listen, to reflect. Let your intention or vision come from within. Ask questions of your inner spirit:

- "What is my focus?"
- "What is mine to do or be?"
- "What is the highest vision for my life?"

Becoming aware of your inner vision and intention takes patience and practice. The more you take time to practice, the more tuned in you will be to the voice of your inner spirit. When your intention or vision is born from within, you'll feel a sense of peace, an aha sensation, a *yes* response from deep within.

2. Shower your intention/goal/vision with positive energy.

In that first rush of knowing, when you're feeling in harmony with your inner spirit, you may feel that anything is possible. Later, doubts may set in as you begin to wonder: "Is this really possible?" "Can I do whatever is required of me on this journey to reach my goal and live my vision?" This is the time to replace those fears and doubts with affirmations or positive thoughts, such as:

- "I can do this."
- "I know what to do and how to do it."
- "I have everything I need to do what is mine to do."

Envision yourself achieving your goal, living your intention, and feeling the joy, fulfillment, and excitement of a well-lived life. Use your affirmations and visions whenever you feel doubt or fear or catch yourself thinking negative words about yourself or the situation.

3. Take the steps you're guided to take.

You may feel unsure of the steps you need to take, but your inner spirit knows exactly what you need to do—one step at a time. The more you relax and trust, the easier it will be to hear and follow its guidance. The more you act on the guidance you receive, the more confident you'll be in following the guidance.

Continue to ask:

- "What step am I to take right now?"
- "Which step will move me in the direction of what I want to be or do?"
- "Which step will bring me the most joy, confidence, and harmony within myself and in my world?"

Take the steps you're guided to take, and observe how you feel and what results occur.

4. Make adjustments as necessary.

Sometimes life throws obstacles in our way. "Keep on keeping on" doesn't mean continuing to push a door until it opens. If you're encountering obstacles on the way to reaching your goal, if you seem to be trying to force an outcome instead of allowing, or if you're feeling frustrated, impatient, or angry with the results you're seeing (or not seeing), it may be time to pause, step back, and reflect on what's occurring. You might want to ask:

- "Is there a better way of reaching my goal?"
- "Is the action I'm contemplating right for me?"
- "What do I need to change in myself to bring about my vision?"

Remember that no step is wasted. What seems to be a misstep may be a lesson you need to learn. A question you may find helpful to ask is, "What have I learned here?" Being willing to see and learn the lessons your journey brings will increase your trust in the process of following your inner spirit.

5. Keep on keeping on.

Keep on in the face of setbacks. Remind yourself of the goal, the intention, the vision. Keep listening. Keep trusting. Keep taking the steps you're guided to take. Keep moving forward even when you feel like quitting. (I've often found the cliché "the darkest hour is just before dawn" to be true when moving through an obstacle in my life.) Persist until the goal/vision is achieved or something better comes about.

Consider that the journey is the destination. As you persist in learning to trust your inner spirit, you gain courage, determination, confidence, patience, and a sense of being in the divine flow of life.

Just as in ballroom dance lessons, sometimes dancing with the Divine is easy, effortless, and fun. Sometimes more concentrated effort and persistence are required. At a time of challenge in my life, my inner spirit spoke loudly and clearly: "*Keep on dancing no matter what! Remember, you're not dancing alone. I am right here with you, leading you in the dance. All you need to do is keep on keeping on following my lead.*"

In our dance with the Divine, let's keep on dancing no matter what happens. Keep on keeping on. Keep on practicing—tuning in, listening, trusting, following. We're always being divinely guided.

Part Four

Living the Dance

Dance is the joy of movement and the heart of life.

– Martha Graham

On our spiritual journey, we are constantly learning and growing. Every experience we have is an opportunity to dance with the Divine. When we follow our inner spirit, our life *becomes* the dance. In our dance, we live the truths we know.

In this book's final chapter, I invite you to consider the truths you know—the truths you're willing to live. I invite you to reflect on the six dance lessons we've learned and how you can live them in your life to create your unique dance with the Divine.

Chapter 11

The Dance Continues

April 30, 2017

What a beautiful spring morning for my last service as minister at Unity of Palmyra! As I drive from my home in New Cumberland to Palmyra, all the pink and white flowering magnolia trees, the bright yellow daffodils blowing in the gentle breeze, and the multi-colored tulips seem to glow in the brilliant sunshine. I'm feeling a sense of joyful anticipation in celebrating my twenty-five years of ministry with my beloved congregation. I'm also feeling a deep sadness in knowing that this will be the last time I'll stand in front of my congregation as their minister.

The day brings a series of small, final steps: being the first to arrive at church, opening the door with the key presented to me when we moved into our building in 2001, greeting our accompanist and song leader and going over some last-minute changes for the service, spending a few minutes before the service in silent prayer in my now nearly empty office, hearing people greeting one another as they gather in the sanctuary.

As I've done so many times before, at 10:25 a.m. I enter the sanctuary from the side door near my office and take my seat beside the pulpit—the exquisite hand-carved pulpit that was lovingly created for me by two very special friends of our congregation. I see the sanctuary filled with my family, friends, and congregation (including some I have not seen for a while but who have come to wish me well on this final Sunday). So much love I see on their faces—all directed toward me. In this moment, all sadness I was feeling dissolves. I feel only love for these dear ones who have trusted me to lead them on their spiritual journeys these many years and who have come to honor and celebrate me today.

I hear the opening chords of "Surely the Presence," one of our congregation's favorite songs, focusing on feeling the divine presence within us and all around us. The service begins. The music and my message reflect the theme for the day: "The Dance Continues."

Just before my message, the congregation joins in to sing the lively, jubilant song, "Life Is a Dance."

> Life is a dance, any way you look at it.
> I know that life is a dance.
> Choose your own partner and pick the best song.
> Come now join in the dance.
> I know that life is a dance.
>
> – chorus from "Life Is a Dance" by Karl Anthony

The Dance Continues

Feeling the lighthearted energy of the moment, I invite my ballroom dance friend Bill to come to the front of the sanctuary and dance with me. On an approximately eight-by-eight-foot carpeted space beside my pulpit, we attempt to execute a Viennese waltz—a very fast, graceful dance with wide-sweeping turns. It isn't a stellar performance by any stretch of the imagination, but my congregation is delighted with this spontaneous addition to the program.

Once again, dancing is reinforcing a lesson I have learned on my spiritual journey: life is a dance, and every experience in life is an opportunity to dance with the Divine. My message reflects this lesson:

> In ballroom dancing, no matter how many lessons I have taken, no matter how many routines I have performed, there is always something more to learn—new steps, new dances, new choreography. In our dance with the Divine, the process of learning to follow our inner spirit is ongoing. Our inner spirit is always moving us in the direction of our highest good—in the direction of growth and unfoldment. Whether following a major transition in our lives—such as graduation, marriage, birth of a child, new job or job loss, retirement, or a challenge overcome—or simply living our everyday lives, the dance continues. No matter what life brings us, our divine partner—our inner spirit—is there to lead us in the dance of life.

At the conclusion of the service, our council presents me with a reddish copper-colored ceramic emblem of an eternal flame inscribed with these words:

> Reverend Julie A. Vance
> 25 Years of Service to
> Unity of Palmyra
> "The Dance Continues"

What a perfect gift honoring the dance we've shared together and a reminder that "The Dance Continues." And so it does.

What's Next?

Sometimes you may have no idea where the dance of life will take you next. But as you continue to practice the dance steps in each of the six dance lessons in this book, you can be certain that your divine partner—your inner spirit—will be leading you every step of the way. You'll notice that your life is flowing more smoothly and easily, you'll feel more confident in the choices you make, you'll develop a greater sense of trust in the guidance of your inner spirit, and you'll observe that your ordinary life is filled with extraordinary synchronicities.

When I retired from full-time ministry, I didn't know what the next few years would bring. But I did know that in making the commitment to continue following my inner spirit, I'd be guided to what was next, one step at a time. What transpired sometimes surprised me, delighted me, or amazed me in the perfect timing and step-by-step process that led me where I needed to be.

To give you an idea of how this process works, I'll share several examples of the six dance lessons working in my life as I continued to follow the guidance of my inner spirit.

Setting the Intention

When I retired from ministry, I insisted that I wasn't really retiring. I set an intention to take a year off to explore who I was at this stage of my life and to discern what my inner spirit was guiding me to do next. (Remember the power of intention?) My inner spirit thought I needed to lighten up, to recapture a feeling of play in my life, to reconnect with friends, to explore what brought me joy. In the spirit of leading and following, that first year was filled with lunches and teas with friends, concerts, the theater, movies, trips to the ocean, yoga classes, and lots of ballroom dancing. I took classes at Pathways Institute and Penn State for those fifty-five years old or older. I explored lighthouses, Islam, spiritual writers, and Pennsylvania artists. Sometimes, even after years of following my inner spirit, I struggled with my nemesis, my inner critic, telling me I really *should* be doing something more productive.

The Lessons Continue

Do you remember a time in your life when you got a job offer or began a relationship and thought, "This happened at just the right time"? After a year off, I was ready to begin venturing back into ministry work. And just then, in perfect divine timing, I was invited to guest speak at Unity of Harrisburg and Unity of Lehigh Valley. My inner spirit led me one step at a time to reconnect with my colleagues in ministry; attend the annual Eastern Region Conference in Charlottesville, North Carolina; and create opportunities to speak and teach classes and workshops at other Unity churches—work that brought me a great sense of fulfillment and allowed me to release my imprisoned splendor.

Next, it was time to practice the lessons of trust and persistence.

In May 2018, I signed up for a class on memoir writing at Pathways Institute. I was convinced that this was the perfect course for me to reconnect with my desire to write a book—although that seemed an improbable dream after so many years of thinking about it but not taking positive action toward it. As soon as I read the description of the class, I felt absolutely sure I was to sign up. One day later, when I registered, the class was filled. I called the registration office, told them how much I wanted to be part of the class, and asked to be on a waiting list in case there were cancellations. I reminded myself that it's all about trust, and if I was meant to be in this class, there would be an opening for me. I kept on keeping on with positive thoughts (and calling the office several times to see if anything had changed). About a week before the class began, I received an invoice with payment for the class requested. To make sure this meant I was really accepted into the class, I once again called the office and heard, "Yes, there's a place for you in the memoir-writing class." Not only did this experience reconfirm that my inner spirit was guiding me through the entire process, but as I shared my writings with the instructor and the class members, the class became a testing ground for my ideas for my potential book. Although only five weeks long, this class was a big step in realizing my dream of writing my own book. Little did I know that two years and many synchronicities later, I would be enrolled in Jodi Chapman and Dan Teck's Your Soulful Book program and well on my way to completing and publishing *Dancing with the Divine.*

Writing this book was the beginning of another journey in my dance with the Divine. I was learning to dig deeper as I discovered tools to bring my writing to life, clarify my ideas, and deepen my trust in my inner spirit. What will be next in my life? Whatever the future brings, I know that it will be a process of leading and following as my inner spirit continues to guide me and I continue to listen to, trust, and follow that guidance.

Practicing the Dance Steps

Practicing the dance steps in each of the six dance lessons in this book is ongoing. As a ballroom dance friend once told me, "Just because you know the dance steps doesn't mean you don't have to keep practicing them."

As we practice the dance steps, we align with the perfect rhythm and order of the universe, we experience greater clarity and confidence in the choices we make, and we feel more in the flow of life. As we review the lessons from this book, consider how they might fit in with your own dance of life.

Leading and Following

When we step back from the busyness of our lives, become still, and listen to the gentle promptings of our inner spirit, we become more in touch with our feelings and needs, more in tune with the gentle (and sometimes annoyingly persistent) leading of our inner spirit, and more willing to trust and follow its lead.

A morning check-in can be a wonderful way to begin your day. Take a few minutes to close your eyes, take a few deep breaths, and/or do a few stretching exercises. You may want to focus on an affirmation or an intention for the day. Ask, "What does my inner spirit want me to know today?" Take a few minutes to be still and listen, allowing your inner spirit to generate any information you need to know for the day. You may find it helpful to write down the response you hear. You may also be guided to take a step moving you in the direction of your intention for the day. If you're guided to take a step, take that step and notice how you feel and the results you experience.

Take time throughout the day to check in with your inner spirit. This can be as simple as pausing for a few minutes from your daily activities, taking a few deep breaths, and asking, "What does my inner spirit want me to know right now?"

Creating time to listen to your inner spirit each day will help you tune in to your inner spirit and to recognize its promptings more easily.

Releasing Our Imprisoned Splendor

Following our inner spirit can lead us to experiences in which we feel most fully alive, are able to be more authentic and honest with ourselves and others, and are best able to express our unique talents, skills, and gifts. We'll discover greater purpose and meaning in our lives. A chance encounter may become an opportunity to discover a lifelong friend or partner. An insight while reading a favorite book or watching a movie may open our mind to possibilities we'd never considered before. Volunteering at a church or retirement community may lead us to a career we hadn't previously imagined.

To discover what helps you release your imprisoned splendor, notice the situations and activities that bring you joy and make time for them.

Share your special talents, skills, and gifts with others. Live in the moment. Pause throughout the day and ask, "What does my body need right now? Which choice will bring me peace right now? How can I be a loving presence right now?"

Live authentically. Speak your truth, not what you think others want to hear. Speaking our truth is the first step in our process toward becoming who we're meant to be. When we're willing to support ourselves by saying, "This is who I am," only then can we expect support from others.

Make choices based on your beliefs and your values rather than blindly following outer rules and shoulds.

Every now and then, step out of your comfort zone. Be willing to try something new; go somewhere you've never been before; look at your life in a new way. Be open to new possibilities for living a joyful, purposeful life—a life in which you find yourself releasing your imprisoned splendor more and more.

Flowing with Divine Timing

As we continue to follow the lead of our inner spirit, we may find that instead of rushing here and there or feeling compelled to follow some arbitrary timing, we move at the pace of our own guidance and accomplish more than we thought we could. My journal entry from September 19, 2018, reflects this feeling:

> My days move more slowly when I move at the pace of guidance. I take time to be still, to watch the sunlight on the trees, the gentle breeze blowing the leaves as I gaze out the window in my meditation room. I needn't hurry. The entire day is before me, open and filled with possibilities.

If you can't imagine a day like this, you might want to consider scheduling an unstructured day, a half day, or a few hours when you have nothing planned and can simply let spirit lead you from moment to moment. Creating time like this reminds us how calm and peaceful it feels when we trust divine timing in our lives.

The Dance Continues

It's All About Trust

Seeing the perfection of divine timing builds trust. We begin to trust that if we ask, we'll receive an answer or a sense of direction. We trust that we're able to follow the guidance we receive. We trust that whatever happens is moving us in the direction of our highest good, even if we can't yet see that good. Often, only in retrospect can we see our experiences from another perspective. We realize that if that new career opportunity, illness, or loss of a relationship hadn't happened, we never would have learned to find the strength within ourselves, the courage to uncover a part of ourselves we hadn't known existed, or the value of living one day at a time.

Reflecting on my own life, I've asked, "How would my life have been different if I hadn't learned to trust and follow my inner spirit?" I probably would have stayed in a marriage that wasn't right for either my husband or me; taught at West Shore until I retired; refused to step out of my comfort zone and travel on my own to Switzerland, Italy, France, and England; pretended I didn't hear the calling to become a Unity minister; and ignored my heart's desire to write a soulful book. I would have led a life that appeared safe and secure, following the shoulds and expectations of others rather than a path that led me to grow, expand, and fulfill my dreams.

To develop trust in following your inner spirit, express gratitude in advance for the fulfillment of your intentions. Act as you are guided even when you don't see how the desired outcome could possibly come about. Expect good to come to you even though it may not appear in the way you anticipate. Be aware of the obstacles to trusting your inner spirit, view them from a higher perspective, and choose a response that moves you forward toward your goal. Practice these steps each day, and before too long you'll find your trust in your inner spirit growing by leaps and bounds.

One Step at a Time—Moving from Fear to Faith

As we continue to listen to our inner spirit and trust its guidance, we discover that most often we're guided one step at a time in the steps we are to take. Although we might prefer to see a blueprint for our entire lives, trusting that we're guided one step at a time gives us freedom from worry and fear. We don't have to figure it all out. We don't have to know how to accomplish that overwhelming project or goal. We only need to take one small step at a time in the direction of our goal. As we take that step, we'll be guided to the next one, and the next, and the next. Each step builds a sense of confidence and trust in the process.

When you're afraid, breathe into the fear, acknowledge what you're feeling, and accept that fear is a part of growth. Focus on the goal or desired outcome. As guided by your inner spirit, take a step—no matter how small the step appears to be—toward the goal or desired outcome. Keep moving forward, one step at a time, asking for help as needed. Feel the power of faith replacing fear as you gain more and more confidence in trusting your inner spirit and following the guidance you receive.

The Dance Continues

Keep On Keeping On

As we persist in our dance with the Divine, we become more adept at recognizing the voice of our inner spirit, more trusting of the process, more willing to follow the steps we're guided to take. We recognize that learning to trust and follow our inner spirit is an ongoing process. Sometimes we move forward with ease and grace, and sometimes we stumble and fall. As we keep on keeping on, we find ourselves experiencing greater peace, harmony, and balance in our lives. More and more, we realize we're never alone; we always have our divine partner guiding us and walking with us on our journey.

Let your inner spirit guide you in setting your intention or vision. Shower that intention or vision with positive energy through affirmations and through envisioning the highest and best outcome. Take the steps you're guided to take. If obstacles seem to be blocking your path, pause to ask whether the action you're taking is right for you or if there's a better way to reach your objective. Be willing to make adjustments as necessary. Keep on keeping on—keep on listening, keep on trusting, keep on taking the steps you're guided to take. Persist until your goal or intention is realized or something better comes about.

WHAT I KNOW FOR SURE

What do you know for sure? Have you ever asked yourself that question? Wouldn't it be wonderful if we could know for sure that our dreams would come true? That we would always have all that we need—time, money, energy? That everything is working for the highest good in our lives?

I believe there is a way we can know all this for sure. We can move from feeling doubt and fear to feeling peace, harmony, and balance in our lives. That certainty and trust doesn't come from outside ourselves, from the rules and expectations of others. It comes from within, from connecting with the deepest essence of ourselves, from knowing that we have an inner spirit that's always guiding us if we're willing to listen, trust, and follow.

As I reflect on my ongoing dance with the Divine, and the lessons in this book that have been part of my journey, I know the following things for sure. I invite you to consider these ideas with an open heart.

1. Each of us has our own special dance.

Music is essential to the dance. In addition to the outer music we hear, within each one of us is our own special music. Dancing with the Divine to our own special music allows us to be the individuals we're created to be.

I've always loved Henry David Thoreau's reference to this inner music in his book *Walden:*

> If a man does not keep pace with his companions, perhaps it is because he hears a different drummer. Let him step to the music he hears, however measured or far away.

As we march to our own drummer—as we dance to our own special music—each of us contributes in our own unique way to

The Dance Continues

the highest good of our world. We each have a purpose for being here on earth, and until we discover and live that purpose through our own unique dance, we will never be truly at peace.

In the book *10 Secrets for Success and Inner Peace,* Wayne Dyer's second secret is "Don't die with your music still inside you." What a powerful message to listen to our inner spirit singing in our ears and express our own special gifts—whether they be teaching, writing, gardening, or simply being a peaceful, loving presence—namely, to release our imprisoned splendor! The more we follow our own special music and trust our inner spirit, the more our path may appear different to others and to ourselves. But as my inner spirit once told me, "*Different does not mean wrong.*"

Throughout this book, I've frequently encouraged you to ask your inner spirit questions to help you gain clarity, to be open to guidance, and to ascertain the next step to take. Now I'm inviting you to consider that your life boils down to a single question—one question that is the theme for your special dance with the Divine. Your life is about dancing with that question. The quality of your existence may well be determined by how well you live in that question. For me, that question has been "How can I learn to listen to, trust, and follow my inner spirit?" For you, it may be "How can I learn to love more fully?" or "How can I find peace within myself?" or "How can I best be of service in the world?" This question may be apparent to you now, or it may take time to uncover. The more you take time to listen to your inner spirit, the more your question and your special dance will unfold for you.

I've found that once I begin to follow my inner spirit, the music becomes louder and clearer. Like a partner in ballroom dancing, my inner spirit begins to gently (and sometimes not so gently) move me in the direction it wants me to go—one step at a time.

2. Our divine partner, our inner spirit, is with us through all the experiences of our lives.

In our lives, our *human* partners may change, but our *divine* partner never changes. Our *awareness* of that divine partner may change as we spend more time consciously connecting with that presence, seeking to be still and listen to the voice of our inner spirit, and trusting the guidance we receive, but our divine partner is always there waiting for our recognition and our intention to connect on a deeper level. This guidance, this voice of our inner spirit, doesn't cease when there's a personal crisis in our lives or a crisis in our world. It grows stronger if we choose to hear it.

During the stay-at-home period of the COVID-19 pandemic in April 2020, when like many others, I was struggling to understand what was mine to do during this time, my inner spirit was reassuring me:

> *Of one thing you can be sure. I am always here for you—to guide you, to comfort you, to reassure you, to lead you in the direction of your highest good. Even though the dance is different in many ways right now, I am still leading you. As always,*

what is yours to do is to follow. Will you dance with me?

When we truly believe we have within us this incredible power—this divine partner that is with us every moment of every day—we know we're never alone. What a comforting feeling!

3. *When we dance with the Divine, every day becomes a celebration of life.*

John O'Donohue's poem "Fluent" captures the feeling of dancing with the Divine as a celebration of life:

> I would love to live
> Like a river flows,
> Carried by the surprise
> Of its own unfolding.

Life does hold many surprises when we dance with the Divine. Each day holds the potential for a new beginning, a new step, a new dance.

In life, we all have experiences of challenges, disappointments, or losses that slow us down or cause us to pause or stop for a while. We need time to reflect, grieve, reconsider. But eventually, the dance of life calls us to move forward and invites us to join the dance. One of the affirmations that spoke to me as I began the new phase of my life—-my new dance—after retirement from ministry was:

> I move forward with positive expectancy as I
> embrace the next years of my life. I continue to

dance with the Divine, and the dance becomes more and more beautiful!

Each day, you might ask yourself, "How will I dance in celebration of myself today?" or "How will I dance with the Divine?" From moment to moment, be aware of what you're feeling, what you're noticing, what's calling to you, what you're guided to be or do. Listen to, trust, and follow the voice of your inner spirit in a celebration of life.

For me, ballroom dancing has been a vehicle for integrating in my body the feeling of dancing with the Divine. I've found that I can experience this same feeling of dancing with freedom and joy through meditation. One morning, I was reading *Falling into the Arms of God: Meditations with Teresa of Avila* by Megan Don. The topic for the day was letting go of expectations of what is to happen during meditation and relying on our inner spirit to guide us where we need to go. The suggested meditation was:

> Relax into the quietness of your being. Lay down your need to control, and agree to let the Divine guide you. Breathe, and trust that you will be taken where you need to go. Breathe deeper and deeper into your being—let yourself go wherever you are being taken.

With gentle music in the background, I relaxed into the present moment and asked my inner spirit to guide me, to take me where I needed to go. I found myself dancing, not with a human partner this time, but dancing through a field of green, leaping into the air, feeling a gentle breeze blowing my hair, feeling free and at ease

The Dance Continues

with myself and with my life. I said to myself, "This is how it feels to dance with the Divine in a dance of life." I could feel the rhythm and harmony of life within me and all around me. I knew that as I focused on that inner presence, I could stay calm and centered within myself no matter what was going on in the world around me.

What a gift to know that each of us has a center within ourselves where we can go and be refreshed and renewed, where we can be guided to what is right for us to do and say at any given moment, where we can let our inner spirit lead us.

I offer here a meditation that may help you experience what it feels like to dance with the Divine. You may want to play background music that feels joyful and flowing. (I love Pachelbel's "Canon in D.")

"Dancing with the Divine" Meditation

Begin by closing your eyes and taking a few deep breaths. With each breath, feel yourself breathing in love, light, peace, and joy. Feel yourself breathing out tension, concern, worry, fear. Breathing yourself into this present moment...

When you're ready, in your mind's eye, allow yourself to dance, even if you have never danced before. Let yourself hear the music within you and begin to dance. Dance with a partner, a child, or a friend, or dance with yourself. Dance in whatever way brings you joy. There are no limitations—just dance! Give yourself all the time you need to enjoy the dance.

And now, no matter whether you are dancing with a partner or without, realize you are dancing with the Divine. You are moving in a divine flow through all the circumstances of your life. Spirit is leading; you are following, moving with grace and ease. You are dancing with the Divine, and you feel wonderful! Continue dancing until your dance feels complete.

When you are ready, bring your awareness back to the present time and place. How do you feel? Take a few minutes to be still and notice the effects.

ARE YOU READY TO DANCE?

Just as my dance with the Divine continues to unfold day by day, step by step, so does yours. When you choose to dance with the Divine, the journey may not always be easy. You will undoubtedly encounter obstacles, doubts, and fears along the way. The twists and turns may surprise you. At times, you may need to summon your inner strength, courage, and resilience to move forward. But I know for sure that with your divine partner—your inner spirit—by your side, you'll never be alone. You'll have all the confidence, courage, and clarity you need to do whatever you're guided to do. You'll feel a greater sense of peace, harmony, and balance within yourself and in your world. You'll feel in the flow of life, moving *with* the river instead of *against* it.

I leave you with these questions:

- "Are you ready to dance?"
- "Will you say yes to your divine partner?"
- "Are you willing to trust your inner spirit to guide you on your pathway through life?"

I hope you'll choose to say yes to your dance with the Divine.

The Dance Continues

May the dance that you choose bring you peace, joy, harmony, balance, and a deeper connection with your inner spirit.

About the Author

Julie A. Vance is an ordained Unity minister, inspirational speaker, workshop facilitator, avid ballroom dancer, and contributing author to the bestselling book *365 Soulful Messages: The Right Guidance at the Right Time.* For the past thirty years, Julie has been committed to trusting her own inner spirit in her "dance with the Divine." Through her classes, talks, and spiritual mentoring sessions, she has delighted in gently guiding thousands of people to discover their own unique dance.

Julie founded and for twenty-five years served as minister of Unity of Palmyra, Pennsylvania. Prior to entering ministry, Julie was an elementary teacher, reading specialist, and owner and founder of Integrity, offering personal and spiritual growth workshops, seminars, and support groups. She received a BS in elementary education from Millersville University and an MEd with reading certification from Shippensburg University.

Julie enjoys traveling, concerts, the theater, a cup of tea and scones at a cozy tearoom, and the freedom and flow of an unstructured day—a day with no schedule or plan, just the opportunity to follow the energy of the moment.

To connect with Julie, for more information on her talks, classes, and retreats, or to download your free copy of her "Dancing with the Divine" meditation, please visit www.julie-a-vance.com.

If you enjoyed this book, please consider writing a positive Amazon review, which may inspire others to learn to recognize, trust, and follow their inner spirit and to dance with the Divine.

Gratitude and Appreciation

To those who have danced with me in creating this book

To Jodi Chapman, Dan Teck, and my fellow writers in the Your Soulful Book program: My inner spirit certainly led me to the right place to write my book. Jodi and Dan, from the moment I received my "welcome packet" of goodies—Your *Bring Your Dreams to Life* book, a dream stone to connect me with my desire to write a soulful book, inspirational cards, two journals, and a personal note—I knew I was exactly where I needed to be, and that I'd be surrounded by love as I brought my book to life. And so I have been—by both of you and by the wonderful group I've been part of for the last two years. Thank you so much!

To Dan Teck, my editor, formatter, coach, and peaceful presence: You've been there every step of the way, supporting me, reassuring me, encouraging me. I've so appreciated your reminders to me that, except for a few hard and fast CMOS rules, I really can trust my inner spirit to guide me in writing this book. Your caring and compassion, coupled with your expertise in all aspects of writing, editing, and publishing, have been a godsend on this journey! I couldn't have done it without you!

To my accountability partner and fellow Your Soulful Book writer, Lorrie Miller, and my longtime friend Kathy Kuser, who read my book chapter by chapter as I continued to reimagine, revise, and reevaluate: Your feedback and encouragement has meant so much to me.

Lorrie, it's been a joy to share this journey with you. I so appreciate the care and attention you have given to providing feedback that has nourished my spirit and encouraged me to keep on keeping on.

Kathy, you've been a confidante, a creative eye, and an intuitive presence for me throughout this journey. Without your prodding me to "dig deeper" when I didn't think I could, your confidence in my ability to let my inner spirit guide me, and your steadfast encouragement, this book wouldn't be as true a reflection of who I am and the message I want to convey.

To my friend and prayer partner, Sharon Marquart, and my new friend Barbara Milbourne, who read my entire manuscript before its release to my editor:

Gratitude and Appreciation

Sharon, your ongoing prayer support as I navigated my book journey and your inclination, as you read my manuscript, to ask questions that gave me food for thought were precious to me. You encouraged me to take risks in sharing my story and to keep on keeping on when I was discouraged and wanted to quit.

Barbara, I so appreciated your willingness to "be the reader who didn't know me." Your perspective as an editor and your insights on my writing helped me reconsider and refine as I moved forward. You've been an unexpected blessing on my journey!

To friends, fellow writers, and students in my classes who've contributed your comments and stories: you've enriched my book by your creativity and unique viewpoints. I appreciate your sharing the wisdom of your hearts.

To the countless friends, family, and colleagues who've cheered me on with your comments, "I can't wait to read your book" and "I know your book will be inspiring": You've helped me maintain my excitement in sharing my book with my readers.

And since, after all, the lessons in this book reflect my ballroom dance experiences, I'm grateful to Deb Davis and Fred Shipley, my dance instructors at Ballroom Break dance studio, for the joy I've experienced in dancing, for your encouragement, and for your friendship. Although I've been doing more writing than dancing these past two years, I haven't forgotten my dance steps!

Made in the USA
Monee, IL
26 September 2022